Timeshare

ALL YOU NEED TO KNOW

Timeshare

ALL YOU NEED TO KNOW

BURT MASON

ROBERT HALE · LONDON

© *Burt Mason 1988*
First published in Great Britain 1988

Robert Hale Limited
Clerkenwell House
Clerkenwell Green
London EC1R 0HT

British Library Cataloguing in Publication Data

Mason, Burt
  Timeshare : all you need to know.
  1. Vacation homes   2. Timesharing (Real estate)
  I. Title
  647'.94   TX303

ISBN 0-7090-3282-X

Photoset in North Wales by
Derek Doyle & Associates, Mold, Clwyd.
Printed in Great Britain by
St Edmundsbury Press Ltd, Bury St Edmunds, Suffolk.
Bound by WBC Bookbinders Limited.

Contents

List of Tables   7
Preface   9

Part One
Thinking About Timeshare

1	What is Timeshare?	13
2	The History	14
3	Size of Market	17
4	The Perceived Pros and Cons	19
5	What is Available?	24
6	Who Uses Timeshare?	33
7	Timeshare Image	36
8	The Future	43

Part Two
Understanding the Structure of Timeshare

9	Legalities	47
10	Licence	50
11	Club Plan	59
12	Legal Procedures (When To Take Advice)	76
13	Disposal	85
14	Costs and Financing	89
15	Comparisons with Other Holidays	97
16	Management Arrangements	104
17	Exchange Facilities	117

Part Three
Choosing Your Timeshare

18	Location – Where Do I Buy My Timeshare?	127
19	What Do I Look For When Buying Timeshare?	131
20	Consumer Protection	142
21	The Developers' Overview	148
22	My Life Style – How Will It Be Affected?	153
23	Questions and Answers	159

Appendices
Useful Addresses	167
What's on Offer in the UK	180
Glossary of Terms and Abbreviations	183
Typical Timeshare Weekly Rental Rates in a High-class Hotel	187
Index	189

List of Tables

Full Home Ownership	22
Packaged Holidays	23
Holiday Points	29
Timeshare Calendar	82-3
Extra Costs: Timeshare versus Outright Purchase	93
Inheritance Tax Rates on Death	94
Transfers made within Seven Years of Death	94
Comparisons with other Holidays: Inflation	97
Comparisons with other Holidays: Timeshare versus 4-Star Hotel	100
Management Charges: Checklist	116
What's on Offer in the UK: Some UK Timeshare Resorts	180-2
Typical Timeshare Weekly Rental Rates	187

Preface

Many claims are made in respect of timesharing and some have fallen short of expectations by a wide margin. Arguably the concept seems to have stood up to the test of time itself since it was first introduced in France in the early sixties, but since then it has suffered from over-zealous marketing which has tended to obscure some of the potential benefits and has resulted in some bad press.

That timeshare will mean many things to many people and will not be compatible with the lifestyle of some is predictable at the outset. This book does not attempt either to justify or condemn but hopefully will give readers a clearer insight on the procedure involved in making a timeshare purchase, highlighting the good points and signposting the dangers so that at the end of the day the readers can decide whether or not it is for them.

Various watchdog committees exist (or are about to emerge) for the purpose of providing consumer protection but so far there is none with teeth enough to police the situation effectively worldwide. Consumers therefore must be educated to the point that they are made aware, through a series of checking procedures, of what is acceptable and what is doubtful. This will enable them to detect the latter, by logically examining the proposition on the offer, and by doing so in a place far removed from the influence of hot sunshine and an excess of hospitality.

For some a timeshare purchase is simply a little flutter; for others it represents a heavy investment of life savings. Like any major purchase, however, it cannot be stressed too often that impartial, professional legal advice should be sought before any commitment is made. All prices and figures quoted in the text are accurate for 1987 and readers should, of course, check them carefully before proceeding. Sadly people are like lemmings on occasions and need to be protected from themselves. Hopefully this book, which cannot possibly cover every aspect of this rapidly changing subject, will nonetheless provide wisdom on the subject through knowledge based on the writer's own experiences over the last five years as a project director for one of the south of England's most successful timeshare developments.

PART ONE
Thinking about Timeshare

1 What Is Timeshare?

Basically timeshare is the means whereby certain facilities are shared between a number of people, the price paid being adjusted according to the amount of time purchased and the time of year. The principle can be applied to almost anything – and indeed you will hear of timeshares in boats, private aeroplanes, a box at the opera or at the races – but for the purposes of this book we are concerned with the timesharing of property and then only in the holiday sense. Whether for reasons of time or financial restraints the concept of being able to buy only what you intend to use has attracted many eager buyers and the market is growing steadily.

One aspect that has added to its appeal is the ability to be able to exchange what you have bought through one of the exchange clubs, thus giving the added dimension of flexibility of holiday choice which is not normally available in buying outright.

2 The History

The origins are and will probably always remain a little obscure but it appears to have begun in France in the 1960s. The French, always a canny lot, came to realize that the cost of a ski chalet could be greatly reduced if this could in turn be shared with Pierre or Philippe or any neighbour of similar persuasion. What therefore started out as an economic necessity developed very rapidly into a business as the field was extended to include villas and apartments at the seaside. Known then as 'multi ownership' (a description that is still used today in Europe and the USA) the concept grew and became accepted throughout Europe until the 1970s when it found its way across the Atlantic to the USA.

Here it found ready acceptance since property developers were having a lean time shifting their inventories due to the very tight clamp imposed by the Federal Bank on loans for second homes. The shift of emphasis onto holiday homes placed purchasing within everybody's reach and, by breaking the segments down still further into single weeks to conform with the American holiday pattern, a breakthrough presented itself.

Developers were able to fill their empty complexes, and buyers found that they had all the amenities of a luxury holiday home without the need for high-interest bank loans and, as an added bonus, all-year-round maintenance. In true American fashion no sooner had 'interval vacationing' arrived than the market was filled with so-called experts, and the selling machine that is the standard tool of all big-time operators took over.

Initially this was led by successful European salesmen but once the techniques were learned the locally bred product took over. Sales schools sprung up all over the country and highly trained teams of salesmen moved from one project to another until sell-out was achieved. Regrettably some of the tactics employed by sales teams, who had been promised additional substantial bonuses by the project developer if sell-out was achieved by certain dates, left much to be desired. This in turn led, after a number of years, to the imposition of tight legislation both by the State and Federal authorities. Nevertheless the interest continued more or less unabated and a multi-million-dollar industry was launched.

In the early days it was the American Sun Belt States of Florida, North and South Carolinas, the Gulf Coasts of Alabama, Louisiana, Mississippi, Texas and the Pacific Coast that saw the timeshare explosion, but now every state in America has its timeshare developments so that even today, when there are some 2,000 resorts in 50 countries operating timeshare, over 70 per cent of these can be found in the USA.

The rapid growth was in part also aided by the American holiday pattern which favoured shorter breaks of seven days taken at more regular intervals and, for the greater part of the 220 million populace, taken in the USA. Americans have rarely left their shores in any numbers and these trips are usually to celebrate retirement or a special visit or reunion with families who have moved, say, to Europe on business postings.

The favourable reaction to the concept of timeshare in the USA placed it beyond all doubt and when it returned to Britain in 1975 ultimate acceptance was assured. The very first timeshare in the UK was created by Frank Chapman at Loch Rannoch in Scotland and the first sale was made by his then Sales Director, Mark Campbell Salisbury – perhaps the doyen, and a much respected figure in the UK timeshare industry.

Sales, painfully slow to start with, gradually 'took off' and Frank Chapman was to create two more resorts before the builder he employed – Barratts – took him over. Progress within the UK may be measured by Chapman's initial efforts which helped to remove doubts in people's minds and pioneered the way for others to follow.

3 Size of Market

The source of statistics used is the returns from the various exchange clubs and the resorts themselves which tend to present information in a form which is difficult to check.

The resorts are eager to demonstrate to their competitors just how well they are doing (if only to spread despondency amongst the opposition!) and sales results quoted are often doubled to shield their real performance.

It is a remarkable feature of the industry that nobody is ever doing badly and enquiries are nearly always greeted with 'fantastic'; 'very buoyant'; 'beating all previous records'; '100 per cent up on this time last year' and so on.

There is ample reason within the industry for optimism and such enthusiastic support is most encouraging but it does make the compilation of any meaningful statistics even more problematical.

More reliable perhaps are the statistics issued by the various exchange clubs but even here there is an area of duplication on the one hand and a shortfall on the other, since the assumption is that everyone buying timeshare automatically becomes a member of one of the exchange clubs. That perhaps is the ideal the clubs would like to see but in reality it does not always happen.

In 1986 there were 1,400 resorts in 40 countries but it would be reasonable to assume that this figure will be comfortably surpassed by the time this book is published. A realistic estimate would put this at some 2,000 resorts in 50 countries.

Again at the last count there were some 40 timeshare resorts in the UK alone and at least 80,000 UK owners,

10,000 of whom own property abroad. In 1975 there was only one resort (Loch Rannoch) and therefore in the relatively short space of eleven years the market has grown 40 times in resort terms.

Because of the conservative nature of the British public the growth has been slower than in the USA but now that the UK has got over its reticence – encouraged no doubt by the entry into the market of big names such as Barratts and Wimpey – steady growth seems assured. Some predict that UK timeshare sales will now double in the next four years, but a more reliable estimate would be a growth rate of 30 per cent per annum.

Timeshare, at least in the eyes of the British, is seen as a viable accepted concept which has stood the test of time itself. Questions of course remain but these are more concerned with the detail rather than the principle.

4 The Perceived Pros and Cons

Generally held views about timeshare itself

The Pros

1. *The exchange facility*   This gives added flexibility to any future holiday plans.
2. *Cost*   They do not have to buy the whole, just a slice they intend to use – so capital outlay is much much less.
3. *Luxury accommodation and location*   Most timeshare is built to a standard which timesharers generally could never afford and in exotic locations. For two weeks in their year they can live a dream.
4. *Consistent standards*   Each year they return expecting to find their timeshare just as they left it (and usually do) – so no worries about any lowering of standards.
5. *All-year-round management*   No risk of vandalism or theft as with wholly owned properties.
6. *Companionship*   Lifetime friendships are struck through frequent returning to the same place.
7. *Reduced risk (investment)*   The capital outlay for the average timesharer is quite small and therefore the risk is minimal while appreciation is almost guaranteed.
8. *Freely assignable licence*   Especially in perpetuity whereby the timesharer knows that the benefits can be passed on. Equally it may be rented or sold without restraint.
9. *Known costs*   Usually the management fees are

geared to the cost of living, and costs can be easily calculated and budgeted for.
10. *Discounted travel* Most overseas timeshare developments have some association with travel companies who offer attractive discounts to regular users. This also applies to car hire.
11. *On-Site amenities* Most timeshares are in leisure complexes or hotels so that very often there is free access to far more than would be available on a package tour.
12. *Ownership* The pride of ownership is a big lure, especially to the timesharer who could never afford to buy outright.
13. *Inflation-proofed holidays* Whilst many good arguments can be made for seeing purchase of timeshare as an investment, most buyers see it as a way of buying tomorrow's holidays at today's prices.
14. *Easily financed* Most schemes offer attractive finance assistance, some aligned with endowment policies which refund (after ten years) more than the purchase price.
15. *Privacy* To be as private as you like or join in – you have a choice.

Sometimes the *pros* can be seen as *cons* and, like beauty, it is all in the mind of the beholder.

The Cons

1. *Reputation* Timeshare seems to attract bad press and there could be a stigma attached to it.
2. *Freedom* They feel restricted by only being able to go at their allotted times of the year.
3. *Trapped* Always see the same people – what a bore – too disciplined.
4. *Cost* Rather go on a package tour as and when we can afford it.
5. *Maintenance* How do we know that standards will be kept up and what about the cost going up every year?
6. *No pets* Not going anywhere without my dog.

7. *Cooking* Not much of a holiday if we have to cook all the time.
8. *Cleaning* Same objection as cooking.
9. *Too risky* All that money at risk if anything goes wrong.
10. *Ownership* If you own any holiday property you become a target for family and friends.
11. *Privacy* We like to be very private when we go on holiday – can't stand crowds or noise.
12. *Health* What if a member of the family is ill and we can't go – what refunds can we get?
13. *Anti-sharing* We don't like to share with anybody.
14. *Investment* Money is better invested in a building society.

So it can be seen that there is wide disparity of opinion at the outset and those attitudes will either harden or soften with experience. Indeed it is not uncommon for people who initially held rigidly to one viewpoint to emerge later in the light of experience as champions of the contrary view.

All fair-minded people will want to compare like with like and the following are the most commonly held and therefore generally most accepted notions of the pros and cons of two distinct styles of holiday – one being the holiday associated with whole ownership and the other the renting of a villa on a packaged holiday.

Full Home Ownership

Although it is reasonable to argue that outright purchase is the better property investment it frequently involves leaving the place unattended for most of the year while still having to bear the full brunt of all repairs and maintenance, some of which of course may be recouped partially through letting. Should you embark on the latter then you should expect accelerated wear and tear on your furnishings and fittings which may then need replacing much earlier.

You will of course have made a higher capital invest-

Pros (timeshare)	Cons (outright ownership)
Owner shares purchase price	Owner bears total cost
May exchange each year for somewhere new	Must use in order to recoup financial outlay
Access to all on-site amenities of a modern resort	Amenities usually fewer and cost more
Luxury furnishings and equipment throughout	Usually furnished to a modest budget
Consistent standards of upkeep	Each visit usually entails more expenditure
All year round management ensures no risk of vandalism	Property at risk through absence of on-site supervision
Financial outlay small – reduced risk	Heavier outlay – possible finance charges
Known costs with management fees fixed to retail price index (RPI)	Costs ever escalating (Rates and community charges)

ment in whole ownership, which means your money is locked in and there is more at risk. For people approaching retirement with a view to the ultimate ownership of a 'place in the sun' then a timeshare acquisition may prove useful in helping them to determine where they want to live, selling it perhaps later once they have made a choice.

Packaged Holidays (Villa – Apartment – Self-Catering)

Pros (timeshare)	Cons (packaged holidays)
Ownership – pride of possession	Non-ownership loss of status
Inflation-proofed holidays with no further outlay	Costs escalate each year
Companionship – friendships created through regular visits	Usually a 'one-off' visit; can be made to feel an outsider
Free membership of local clubs through ownership	Not normally available when renting
Standards known in advance	An element of taking 'pot luck'
Discounted travel gives further cost reduction	Not normally available when buying package
Confidence in on-site management/standards	Unknown quantity puts holiday at risk

5 What Is Available?

To say you are spoiled for choice would be something of an understatement since, by the time you read this, there will be well over 2,000 resorts to choose from in 50 countries with over 40 of these in the UK alone. Bringing it closer to home there are now 400 resorts in Europe and the growth rate is now approaching that of the mid-1970s in the USA.

Breaking it down into types and styles of timeshare in the market we find that there are three packages which seem to find most favour and these are:

1 Community Timeshare

This is where a collection of lodges, villas or apartments are built around a central administration block with shared amenities, such as swimming pools, restaurants, sports facilities, shops, theatres and in some cases even on-site medical facilities. A village (pueblo) atmosphere is created and this type of timeshare is strong in appeal for those who like a social life and take security from the safety-in-numbers aspect.

Langdale and Lakeside Village in the Lake District are two popular examples of this type in the UK whilst Marbessa Village and El Capistrano on the Costa del Sol are good examples in Spain. Just as whole property owners abroad tend to favour community developments so does this trend prevail with some timesharers. Properties offering this form of timesharing can be found in every country where timesharing is being sold – and it holds a dominant place in the market.

2 Hotel Based

This is where a section of a hotel is operated on a timeshare basis with all the amenities of the hotel being available to timesharers without any additional cost. Since most hotels, according to their rating, offer a host of services and amenities, this particular form of timeshare appeals to those seeking the privacy of their own suites yet wishing to leave them at will, free to join in the entertainments provided.

In the main these timesharers are more individualistic and less attracted to the community way of life. The Osborne in Torquay, the Carlton in Bournemouth and the Craigandorrach in Scotland are good examples of this style of timeshare in the UK.

Hotel-based timeshare is more popular in Europe and it is only possible to list a few examples here, such as the Hotel Panoramic in Villars, Switzerland; the Schloss Grubhof in Lofer, Austria; the Grand Hotel Emma in Merano, Italy; the Madeira Beach Club in Funchal, Madeira; and the hotel Guadalmar in Malaga, Spain.

Many hotels have found it possible to combine the hotel and timeshare activities since every week, almost regardless of the season, it has a pre-set occupancy level around which (since most timesharers eat in their restaurants and drink in their bars) they are able to plan their staffing levels. Indeed without timeshare residents many of these hotels would be obliged to cut back on staff and services quite drastically during the winter months.

3 Club-Style Timeshare

There are many timeshare developers who have found it advantageous to operate a club style of timeshare and a large proportion are based on fine old houses or castles. Although, like hotels, they offer many amenities, principally restaurants, tennis, golf and a health spa, they are open to the locals who can gain access to these amenities by becoming a member. Although this ensures a profitable operation for the developer the sheer weight of membership can result in some inconvenience for the timesharer, but it must be remembered that fine old houses require an enormous amount of annual expenditure to ensure survival and the funds for this cannot be solely recovered from the timesharers.

Some of the early developers of this style of timeshare rapidly sold out of the available accommodation in the house itself and extended the operation by building villas and lodges in the grounds (Broome Park and Elmers Court are two examples). Somehow the appeal of 'owning' part of an historical building diminishes when it becomes a modern lodge or villa in the grounds, particularly when the hospitality centre is the house and you have to brave the elements to get there.

You will no doubt be aware of (and perhaps even confused by) other schemes in existence which are strictly speaking not timeshare but tend to become associated with it in some people's minds when comparisons are being made. Some explanation of these now follows in the interest of presenting a complete overview.

Co-ownership

They say that everything runs in cycles and this now seems to be true in timeshare as more and more buyers (having perhaps tested the timeshare concept and decided that this is the life for them) are turning to a bigger slice of ownership. So the concept of multi-ownership, which seriously began back in 1962 before becoming more fragmented and emerging as timeshare, now appears to be finding favour once more as co-ownership.

By this we mean that the buyer agrees to purchase a quarter, a sixth or even an eighth of the total and that this rotates usually month by month, each year with the other owners (for example, January and February one year, March and April the next, or January and July, followed by February and August). Generally this form of purchase has more appeal to those approaching retirement who, for a relatively small investment, want to sample the environment before becoming more directly involved. Or it will have appeal for those who, having owned outright for a period of years, now prefer the split-ownership arrangements as the best of both worlds.

After all if there are seven other owners it is usually possible to find one with whom you can swap if one year your time allocation is inconvenient. Then there is the question of cost – the uplift on the overall outright purchase price is marginal compared with the accepted uplift on timeshare so co-ownership is proportionally cheaper and in some schemes there are still the opportunities for exchange through affiliation with the exchange clubs.

Another attractive feature is that for those who waver between timeshare and the outright purchase of a rather modest villa or apartment, co-ownership enables them to raise their sights considerably and, for approximately half that which they would have spent on outright purchase, buy a quarter share in something altogether more lavish and prestigious.

Of course it must be remembered that a larger share brings with it a bigger share of the costs and these need to be looked at very carefully with inflation in mind. So too must the legal title so that in the event of your wanting to sell you do not find yourself having to wait for the whole to be sold before you can receive your money.

Usually these arrangements are for a fixed period of say twenty years after which the property is sold and each co-owner receives an equal share of the proceeds. If someone backs out in the interim then either the others can buy him or her out or, in some instances, the onus is on the person backing out to find a replacement.

The number and variety of such schemes is prolific, which is perhaps in itself a fair indication that there is a high level of interest in this form of ownership. The success or otherwise depends entirely on just how compatible the other owners are. The fewer owners the better in respect of reaching agreement on issues but then again your share of the costs is that much greater.

Many of course are privately launched as the brainchild of a neighbour or friend with whom you have similar interests and invariably these are the first to come unstuck because not enough research has gone into them or not enough is known of the legal structure in the country of purchase. If you are tempted by any of these schemes then do insist on talking personally to the lawyers involved and have a qualified person check out the documentation.

Gaining full undisputed ownership of property abroad can be difficult enough as a lone buyer let alone the complications of there being four or more. On balance you will probably be better placed if you make your judgment uninfluenced by friendships and through a company specializing in this type of activity.

Even so you should sign nothing until your solicitor has had a good look at the proposition. Remember, however, that if there are eight of you involved then you will need everything to be decided in committee and that might be very frustrating for some.

The Holiday Property Bond

The Holiday Property Bond (HPB) is issued by Isle of Man Assurance Ltd and marketed in the UK by its agents, Villa Owners Club Ltd.

Launched some six years ago the HPB is claimed to be a tax-efficient way of investing in property and to join the scheme you make a lump-sum investment in a life assurance policy. Your money is then partly invested on holiday property, which through a points system you may use rent-free for your holiday(s) each year, and partly in securities. The income from these securities is then used in the running and maintenance of the properties.

The argument put forward is that you have the benefits of property ownership without the worry or costs of maintenance – no management fees are charged. It is also claimed that unlike timeshare you may have the use of the property at any time of the year. At present however there are not many properties and much will depend on when you apply and when you want to go.

So how does it work?

For the money invested in HPB you will receive an

Thinking About Timeshare

annual allocation of 'holiday points' which you use to book the holiday property of your choice. Each property has its own holiday-points value for each week of the year. For instance, a large villa in high season is clearly going to need more points than a one-bedroomed apartment out of season. A holiday-points chart which is revised quarterly shows the number of points needed for each holiday week in each property.

At present there are properties in Spain, Portugal, The Canaries, Cyprus, Austria, France and the UK but others are planned and no doubt as the number of investors grows so the funds will be available for additional purchase. The emphasis is placed on booking early to ensure you get the property you want.

The minimum premium is £1,000 and this may be topped up in increments of £250. A typical example is shown in the table. A pound sterling is equal to one holiday point.

Time of year	Examples (£5,000 investment)	Holiday points
Mar. 1987	2 weeks at Playa Bastian (Lanzarote) for 4 persons	3160
Nov. 1987	1 week at Barnham Broom (Norfolk) for 6 persons	1770
		4930*

* The remaining 70 points are carried over into 1988

You may continue to add to your points holding over the years until you have arrived at the pattern that best matches your holiday requirements. Meanwhile you receive life assurance and there is a buy-back guarantee after two years if you decide to leave.

A new option introduced is that members can become Gold Bondholders which gives them 50 per cent more holiday points. In return they agree to pay a 'user charge' each time they use a property, which is seen by some members as a thinly disguised management fee and is therefore in conflict with one of the original benefits that no management fees are charged.

The purpose is clearly to raise more funds for property purchase and the reasoning is that if Gold Bondholders accept user charges then less need be invested in securities (necessary, it was originally argued, to earn income to pay for the maintenance) and more in properties. On the other hand it might just be that the revenue from investments is falling short of the sums needed to sustain the properties in prime condition.

In all fairness it must be said that existing and future bond owners may stay as ordinary holders (now regarded as in the silver category) and not pay user charges – thus foregoing the 50 per cent holiday-point bonus. Villa Owners Ltd Managing Director, Geoffrey Baber, states that 61 per cent of bond owners have already opted for 'Gold'. Typical user charges are as follows:

Spain	– £45.59	Cyprus	– £45.55	Austria	– £69.00
Norfolk	– £59.69	Portugal	– £69.00	Scotland	– £49.50

It is anticipated that the present 2,000 bondholders will double during 1987. A recently completed survey of preference for purchases in new locations amongst bondholders shows an overwhelming choice of Florida as the most preferred (19.4%), with the Dordogne (9.8%) South-West England (9.5%), Tuscany (9.5%) and the Italian Lakes (9.1%) being next in line.

Of the existing locations preferred, the Algarve and Brittany were almost equal first choice with Cyprus and Lanzarote next.

The success of the HPB will depend on the provision of more properties of quality and style in exotic locations with full on-site amenities and their ability to maintain these adequately out of the funds available, without surcharges. The customer profile appears to be the same as that of timeshare and many bondholders are already timesharers who will be in a position to make valid comparisons. The acid test will be: will these stand up and

Thinking About Timeshare

if they do then there is no reason why the current rate of growth should not continue.

Holiday Clubs – Hapimag

Another variation is the holiday property club operated by Hapimag of Switzerland. Established in 1963 Hapimag is a non-profit making club owned exclusively by its members of which there are now over 43,000. Its main purpose is to buy holiday properties for use by members, their families and friends.

In addition Hapimag provides extensive holiday services of high standard. The club offers the benefits of holiday freedom coupled with the economics of leisure property ownership. Simply put it is a form of holiday home ownership as an alternative to mass tourism.

From its modest beginnings in 1963 its holiday property portfolio is now estimated to be worth more than £150M. There are forty or more holiday locations, mainly seaside, ski resorts and in the country or in capital cities. Spread over eleven countries these include Austria, Denmark, Finland, France, Germany, Greece, Italy, Spain (including the Ballearics and the Canaries), Sweden, Switzerland and the UK. Add to this the world-wide facilities for exchange through Resort Condominiums International (RCI) and one begins to appreciate the scope of the operation.

It is claimed that you may choose the size and style of accommodation, ranging from two to seven persons in either hotel or as self-catering. Furthermore you may have more than one holiday each year and if you cannot take up your entitlement this may be accumulated for up to five years.

The minimum investment, which buys you twelve points, is 4,900 Swiss Francs and this entitles you to up to three weeks holiday each year in perpetuity. Other charges are an annual fee of currently 156 Swiss Francs, which is partly for the upkeep of the properties and partly for the management and services, the latter at cost.

Surprisingly perhaps, Hapimag, which surely has enough to offer in its own right and follows very closely the timeshare concept, has seemingly sought out timeshare as its main opposition in its sales brochure which publishes a questions and answers comparisons list.

The message it contains (if there is a message) is confused and their conclusion is that 'Hapimag is for those who love variety and change whilst having an eye for long-term financial benefits.' They have also assessed timeshare as being suitable for those 'who wish to visit the same resort at the same time annually such as skiers and lovers of the Riviera as well as holiday makers who wish to see the same friends every year.'

6 Who Uses Timeshare?

The answer to this must be almost anyone who is eager to have a guaranteed holiday year in year out without any of the risks in determining choice of resort and when to go there.

Obviously the type of customers attracted to each resort will vary. Some will have a predominance of professional people such as doctors, solicitors, accountants, stockbrokers, bankers and businessmen, while others will have a wider cross section including farmers, hoteliers, garage proprietors, builders, younger executives, civil servants and even politicians.

Much will depend on the resort location, the amenities it offers and its local attractions, such as beaches, shops, museums, places of historic interest, sporting facilities and general environment. But in the main those attracted to the luxury resorts will have accrued disposable incomes over a period of years and now, with both money and time available, they are eager to invest in a lifestyle that has long been their goal.

Most have grown-up families which are now 'off their hands', leaving them free to plan their personal leisure time without restrictions. All appreciate that good health is not a gift for ever and they are determined to get the best out of life while they can. They tend to look for the ultimate in luxury both in standards of accommodation and support services. Price is seldom an obstacle once they are convinced that the resort offers all that they seek plus sound management security.

That then is one category but at the other end of the scale is the younger buyer in the process of raising a family which is yet too young to travel. In the main these buy into UK timeshare and seek periods which coincide with school holidays.

In between these are those whose families are of an age when travel is less prohibitive and who nearly always holiday abroad once in the year. They have been quick to accept the savings offered by timeshare against the more traditional package holidays and there can be little doubt that this market is under increasing threat from the growth of timeshare.

In spite of the great shadow of unemployment (or maybe even because of it) there is more and more leisure time available now that six week holidays (including statutory) have become the norm rather than the exception. Most families plan a family holiday, be this at home or abroad, and this takes two weeks. They then take a break in the spring (Easter or spring bank holiday time) or in the autumn. Most of industry extends the close-down at Christmas to a two-week break and those periods are very popular with timeshare purchasers in the UK.

The ease of being able to jump into a car and in a matter of hours starting your holiday takes preference for these shorters breaks over all the problems of air travel. This then is the hard core of the business sustaining the UK timeshare developers.

For all categories however timeshare represents a dream holiday with luxury standards (even opulence) that cannot be repeated at home, in prestigious developments and in exotic locations. To this you can add pride of ownership which may account for the fact that most timesharers are pleasantly surprised when returning year after year to find things exactly as they remembered them. In this sense at least timeshare cannot be compared with normal holiday letting where furniture and fittings come in for some very harsh treatment indeed. It is simply that if you 'own' something you look after it.

People too are attracted, particularly in the small resorts, to the exclusive club atmosphere which seems to prevail, and lasting friendships are being developed both with the management and other timesharers. If it is in a hotel location the staff are quick to realize that the timesharer is a long-term 'regular' customer and they make a point of learning their likes and dislikes and treating them with great deference, so that far from being a second-class citizen in such an establishment, which might have been in their thoughts (but nobody else's) when they purchased, they become instead distinguished guests.

This experience invariably prompts them to extend their holding beyond their initial purchase and it is recorded that one hotel timesharer has now purchased no less than twenty weeks having started with eight – a virtual home from home for him, his family and friends. Another guest, who had been coming to the hotel man and boy for fifty years, bought timeshare because 'he had been so much a part of the hotel's history that he wanted to be part of its future'.

Go to any cocktail party and you will find that the most surprising people own timeshare and given the opportunity are only too pleased to talk about it. At a recent party I attended, out of the sixty guests no fewer than ten owned timeshare and one of these was a QC whilst another was a university professor.

The appeal therefore covers a wide spectrum and as it becomes evident that the concept works in practice the numbers are growing.

7 Timeshare Image

To some it may seem that the media unfairly pounce on the bad experiences related to timeshare whilst ignoring the many thousands of satisfied users but that is the 'dog bites man' syndrome of reporting – 'man bites dog' will always get better coverage. Each year for example the travel trade sends millions of customers on holidays, the vast majority of whom return full of praise for the transporter, the hotel, the food and the resort.

Occasionally someone gets a raw deal, a delayed flight, an overbooked hotel, indifferent food and perhaps a snatched handbag incident to boot. In percentage terms it is infinitesimal but such instances are again widely reported. So it is with timeshare – most developers have files bulging with highly complimentary letters going back over many years but occasionally someone has cause to complain and that gets reported.

In fairness it must be said that the more responsible press have generally come to accept that timeshare is here to stay and that some highly reputable companies are the hard core of the industry. There is now less 'knocking' and more support from the media as the industry, ever conscious of its image, strives to clean up its act.

This is not to say that there are no rogue elements in existence whose only purpose is to sell quickly and get out. They do this by employing large sales teams who move from project to project, using high-pressure sales techniques backed up by hordes of commission agents who roam the streets, beaches, hotels, airports and restaurants offering every inducement under the sun to prospective buyers to view.

Thinking About Timeshare

These are usually students who are flown out from the UK and paid handsomely for each couple who accept an invitation to view. Having paid for the introduction the sales process is already under pressure to produce the results and the couple are exposed to every trick in the book to make them buy. Anyone not buying is often abused, insulted and made to feel inadequate – particularly when, in a husband and wife partnership, one is in favour and the other against.

Many a nice holiday is spoilt because an insensitive salesman has caused a rift between couples due to one or the other failing to accept his arguments.

These tactics are deplorable and happily the countries harbouring such companies are responding to pressures to have them stopped: it is becoming so bad that holidaymakers cannot leave their hotels without being accosted by several commission agents in quick succession – each more aggressive than the last. The countries themselves are only too aware that unless these tactics are effectively stopped then they could have serious repercussions on their holiday industry.

Such tactics however only succeed because people themselves allow them to. There is only a certain margin to be made on a timeshare sale and any free gifts, discounts, meals or champagne drunk is going to have to come out of that margin. If the sales costs are high – as indeed they are in such situations – then the project has to be paid for over and over again out of ever-increasing maintenance costs.

That is not to say that reputable companies never offer a discount – they do, but it is more important that you satisfy yourself about the reason for the discount. A good test is to look for a discount on two weeks or more: if none is forthcoming then you can feel secure since the developer is demonstrating his strength in the market place.

The concept of timesharing has already drawn buyers from all walks of life and such buyers will fiercely protect their decision from any critics. This loyalty is borne out of experience and it is a fact that the critics are those who have no valid experience and adopt a view similar to that so aptly expressed in the Guinness advertisement – 'I don't drink Guinness because I've never tried it.' The diehards will of course never buy but, as the growth statistics show, more and more each year are beginning to appreciate the attractions.

Developers can gracefully accept most reasons for not buying but sometimes it is particularly hard to see a middle-aged couple who have worked all their lives to bring up a family, provide them with a good education, help them financially to get a start in life and then be deprived of something they have set their hearts on by the selfishness of their offspring.

There have been countless examples of couples in their mid-fifties viewing a luxury timeshare in the UK and relishing the prospect of ten to fifteen years enjoyment in the Indian Summer of their lifetime. Such couples have usually travelled widely and have lost some of their earlier enthusiasm for travelling abroad. They might also have a recurrent health problem which restricts their mobility and gives them another reason for avoiding the hassles of overseas travel.

With their minds made up they pay their deposits and return home full of excitement for their purchase. Naturally they discuss it with their family and some days later telephone to say that their sons and daughters prefer an overseas location and they have to cancel.

Often the overseas purchase is an outright buy of a villa or apartment in Spain or Portugal – a much higher capital outlay so that the 'family' can have all the year round use of it. Sadly the parents often never even go there: it is too hot or too far or too tiring; there is no peace and quiet with all the children around. So their dream has been dashed simply because their children looked only at the benefits to themselves and ignored completely the wishes of the parents.

Some readers of this book may have experienced this and if so they will know that given the same situation again their reactions would be very different. Parents buy timeshare in the knowledge that ultimately their children will inherit the benefits as part of the estate but they have a right of choice and – as they are usually paying – the right to benefit during their lifetime.

Sadly, the industry itself is largely to blame for not making better use of the enormous fund of goodwill that already exists amongst its one million or so timesharers, the majority of whom have steadily increased their own holdings of timeshare weeks over the years simply because of their entire satisfaction with their original purchase and the services they have received.

Many of these are excellent ambassadors and referrals feature highly amongst sources of new business. Of their own accord a great number have written letters of commendation. Naturally developers will want to protect the identity of their timesharers but enthusiasm is so high that a large percentage of satisfied owners would gladly give permission for their views to be made public. Some are more than happy to be interviewed on video or on radio chat shows – they are just waiting to be asked.

Of course there are developers who have made and continue to make full use of their public relations opportunities to promote a better image for the industry but their efforts need to be collated into a national or even international campaign working to clear objectives and supported by an adequate budget. Success should be highlighted and when this has been given appropriate exposure it will serve immeasurably to counteract some of the adverse reporting encountered from time to time.

So much for the industry's failure to recognize the benefits of its customers' opinions. What about the timesharers themselves – how do they view their status as timesharers?

It would be fair to say that at one point there was a certain stigma attached to owning timeshare which was regarded with suspicion by those who perhaps failed to understand its place, poised as it is between outright ownership and self-catering holidays. To those yet to experience the benefits the whole thing seemed too good to be true and therefore stretched credibility.

Many a conversation on the subject of proposed holidays ended in raised eyebrows at the mention of two weeks timeshare in Torquay, particularly when the enquirer was off to the Bahamas for the umpteenth time.

Over the years however this has steadily changed as timesharers have made use of their exchange facilities and talk from experience of holidays in Hawaii or Fiji and other exotic locations – and at a fraction of the cost.

So what has brought about this shift of opinion? Well, simply that there are more highly thought of members of our society buying timeshare today and their opinions and reactions to their experiences tend to carry weight in any argument. We often hear related at our clubs or gatherings the experiences of a number of people, whom we respect, following an initial first-time occupancy or an exchange and they nearly all have the same note of satisfaction prevailing.

For those of us who may be simply interested bystanders such tales will stick in our memories for a variety of reasons, each with their own individual appeal – exotic locations, luxury standards of accommodation, the weather, sporting facilities or the economy of it all. Such chance conversations are all playing their part in making people think more objectively about timeshare, just as a bad experience related in detail to a large enough audience would have quite the reverse effect.

To many it seemed that with the advent of timeshare the whole holiday industry had been 'turned on its ear' and that things would never quite be the same again. It can be realistically argued of course that out of a population of some 57 million a mere 80,000 or so owners of timeshare in the UK is a drop in the ocean but it could also be the tip of the iceberg – where those have gone others seem certain to follow.

In the concluding chapters of this book I deal a little more with the impact on lifestyle of a successful timeshare purchase, but I would also like to mention here one other benefit that adds to the status of owning timeshare and that is 'ownership'.

Some good friends recently returned from a holiday in Portugal where they had been offered, and gratefully accepted, the use of a neighbour's villa complete with car, located in the hills above Villamura. There were the inevitable flight delays and they were three hours late into Faro. In the gathering gloom they found their car, a

Thinking About Timeshare

rapidly rusting Mini, in the car park.

Even with the aid of the roof rack they found it quite impossible to pack in all of their luggage and eventually, to cries of protest from their two children, were forced to leave one case – theirs – behind in the baggage handling department of Air Portugal. This finally resolved they drove, albeit somewhat precariously, out on to the main arterial coastal road.

After some thirty minutes they found their turn-off and now on the last lap commenced their steep climb up an unmade road. Half way up, the heavily laden car bottomed out and the silencer was ripped off so that they continued the rest of their journey sounding like a formula 1 Grand Prix car.

Under the gaze of startled neighbours they found their villa and unloaded the car which in the last half mile had commenced to boil. By now they were too tired to care and doing their best to ignore the scurrying cockroaches they found their respective bedrooms and called it a day.

The villa had a pool and they relished the thought of a swim before breakfast. Unfortunately the water was a very murky green and quite stagnant, the level was two feet below normal and the debris floating on the surface made it singularly unattractive. Also in March, it was bitterly cold.

To cut short the saga, they spent most of their holiday cleaning out the pool finally ordering and paying for a tanker delivery of fresh water (together with some very expensive chemicals to ensure the correct balance), repairing the car, repairing shutters that had been forced in an attempted break in, and generally getting the place ready for the letting season to follow.

What then had been planned as a nice relaxing Easter with the children, in the sun and all for free except for air fares, proved to be quite the opposite. They absorbed the costs of repairs to the car (a new exhaust system, a head gasket plus radiator thermostat, and a roof rack) as well as all related expenses in the villa, and after presents for their neighbour's children they found that their 'free' holiday had cost more than the average good-class package tour.

The terms 'idyllic and charmingly rustic' sound good in

any sales prospectus but the truth of the matter is that they normally mean 'remote, isolated and miles from anywhere' which has to be measured against the facilities one enjoys in a properly run leisure complex where every amenity is to hand.

I suppose the warning bells should start to ring when someone says, 'You may have to rough it a bit,' or 'After all it's not a hotel and there are things you may have to do for yourself.'

How nice then when you are in a position to repay some of this hospitality and to watch the growing appreciation in your friends' eyes as they come to grasp the value of a fully managed, well maintained and serviced property with many on-site amenities thrown in. Is it little wonder that one of the biggest sources of new business for timeshare comes from a disillusioned band of outright owners many of whom go on to become the holders of multiple weeks?

8 The Future

Perhaps the most comforting thing for would-be investors in timeshare is that it was not a sudden success. People needed convincing – and indeed still do – that the concept was solidly based and that the market would continue to expand. Traditionally the UK market response has been cautious, as it is with any new approach to established patterns of behaviour.

Timeshare introduces a new discipline in that it requires an annual commitment to a specific time each year, even though this can be made more flexible by using the exchange facility. For those running their own businesses, this comes as a blessing, since it encourages them to take holidays that might otherwise be brushed aside because of other pressures.

The fluctuations in the fortunes of the pound and the resultant higher travelling costs by air are making family holidays abroad, even on package terms, a factor to be reckoned with in the future, and the annual family package holiday 'two weeks in the sun' is likely to be less frequent than in the past as it gives way to timeshare.

Because of this and the adverse publicity some European tourist areas are receiving in relation to criminal acts that seem to go unchecked, timeshare is fast becoming a serious contender to the travel companies, forcing them in turn to be more selective in the holidays they offer.

It is a mistaken conception that timesharing will only appeal to those people interested in self-catering, since whilst most timeshare units offer luxury kitchens as standard, the truth is that these are seldom fully utilized.

Many will have bought timeshare imagining perhaps that they would cater for themselves, but by the second day of their stay they can be found in the restaurants and bars enjoying all the benefits of not having a hotel bill to pay for accommodation when they check out.

There are, of course, changes within the timeshare industry itself, since initially it was thought that to enjoy the attractions of the many resorts on offer, it was necessary to buy in several locations. Now, with the advent of Resort Condominiums International (RCI) and other exchange clubs, the pattern has been to buy in your favourite resort and exchange into the others as the mood takes you. There is, as a result, a flurry of resale activity as owners sell in other locations and concentrate on buying more, usually the same weeks, in the resort of their final choice.

To those outside the industry this can mistakenly look like a disenchantment with their purchase, more especially so in the development where they are selling as the real purpose is not always stated, but in reality it is simply that they have 'grown up' with the industry and are consolidating their position.

Also, late entries into the market are setting standards of accommodation and amenities which hitherto did not exist and this in itself is the cause of some restlessness amongst previous owners.

The concept itself, however, is standing up well, and this is reflected in the customer profile for each resort. It can be anticipated that as far as the UK is concerned the market will grow rapidly in terms of timesharers, but remain more or less static in terms of developers – in short a lot more business will be shared between the existing operators as the market requirements are met.

PART TWO
Understanding the Structure of Timeshare

9 Legalities

It is a daunting task for any layman to write about the law and therefore I believe it is prudent to prefix this section by stressing yet again the need to take qualified legal advice before entering into any commitment in timesharing, or for that matter any of the closely related schemes covered in the preceding pages.

For those who want to delve further into the legal implications of timesharing James Edmonds's excellent book *International Timesharing* (2nd edn) is available at around £20. It is a lawyer's guide to the whole complex business of international law in its application to timesharing.

For the purpose of this book however we can do no more than scratch the surface.

If we accept that the anti-perpetuity laws of England and Wales and the Law and Property Act 1925 make the transfer of the freehold in property in undivided shares a non-starter as far as timeshare is concerned, then there remain four basic methods of buying timeshare in the UK.

1. **Lease**
   The timesharer is granted a discontinuous lease from the developer in the same way as a normal landlord/tenant relationship. This applies very rarely.

2. **Licence**
   The timesharer is given a 'right to use licence' for a given period, after termination of which the property reverts to the developer.

3. *Company purchase*
   This assumes that the timesharers become shareholders of a vested public limited company – another rarely used system.

4. *Club plan*
   This can either be a proprietary club or a members' club, the basic difference being that the developer retains title in a proprietary club and grants membership to the timesharers, while in a members' club the members become the owners, the extent of their ownership being governed by their level of purchase.

   Although on the face of it this may appear attractive, it must be remembered that ownership brings with it the responsibility for maintenance and general upkeep so that enthusiasm for the project tends to fade with the arrival of bills for repairs and associated costs after several years experience.

Timesharers are often confused by the bewildering array of documents produced in support of some club plans and it is sound advice to have these checked by your solicitor: do not sign anything that might be a commitment until you have.

It is truly amazing how often this advice is totally ignored in the face of high-pressure salesmanship but the more you are pressured for an instant decision the more you should suspect the proposition. After all, any reputable company will incorporate a 'cooling-off' period of ten days while you get your thoughts together and take legal advice – if it's for life, what's the hurry?

We must recognize that timeshare is still relatively new and that in the property market terms twenty or so years is only a drop in the ocean. Because it is so new, each year sees some new development and change in legislation which could become mandatory under the laws of the country.

It is not the purpose of this book to advise on matters so deep and complex – that is a job for your solicitor. Instead I will attempt to throw light on what the various methods

Understanding the Structure of Timeshare

of purchase entail and to increase the reader's overall appreciation in this elementary context.

It might at this stage be helpful to know that in the UK interests in property are divided into legal estates and equitable estates. The reasons are largely historical and are governed by the Law of Property Act 1925. Under Section 34 (2) of this Act the provision is made

> that where land is expressed to be conveyed to any persons in undivided shares and those persons are of full age, the conveyance shall operate as if the land has been expressed to be conveyed to the grantees, or, if there are more than four grantees then to the first four named in the conveyance as joint tenants upon the statutory trusts.

In layman's terms what this means is that if there is an attempt to convey freehold land to more than four timesharers the legal title will rest with the first four named and the remainder will have only an equitable interest which can be over-reached by any of the first four named.

So if you are offered timeshare in England or Wales on a freehold basis, be instantly on guard or you might find that you have no legal title at all.

10 Licence

In practice the most commonly used method of selling timeshare in the UK is by licence. This means that the developer who has legal title to the property grants the timesharer a right to use licence for the weeks purchased by them throughout the lifetime of the agreement.

This is (or should be) freely assignable and the timesharer may authorize others to use it unrestrained (beyond, that is, in compliance with the standards of behaviour required by the developer); they may sell it, bequeath it or even give it away.

Even though the terms of the licence should be spelt out very clearly in the agreement, there are still some doubts remaining in the timesharer's mind about its implication. It may vary with development but in general terms it means that the timesharer may enjoy all the amenities of the resort during the period in residence.

Some timesharers return to the resort during the summer months, stop at a nearby hotel with little or no amenities and then present themselves with their friends at their resort and proceed to lay claim to the available sunbeds around the pool as if they were in residence. When challenged they hotly declare that they are entitled to do this under the terms of their agreement.

Allowing once again that some resorts will accept this the greater majority do not and are obliged to turn away non-resident timesharers in favour of those in residence. It is not therefore an inherent right and, although out of season this might not be a problem for the resort, in season it most certainly is, and timesharers should understand it.

Understanding the Structure of Timeshare

Worst still, there have been exchange club members, not on an exchange, who have imagined that their exchange club membership automatically gives them the right to use the amenities at any affiliated resort whether they are owners at that resort or not.

This of course could not be further removed from reality since there is nothing assumed or implied in any of the exchange clubs' membership terms to this effect. Such a misunderstanding, I believe, has arisen largely because some resorts have adopted the practice of seeking to boost turnover at quiet times of the year by encouraging exchange club members to use the amenities and falsely informing them that they are entitled to do so under the terms of their club membership.

All licences will have been structured to reflect the interests of both developer and owner and a typical licence is reproduced here, unedited, with the kind permission of the Carlton Hotel. The only omission is the front page containing the particulars.

THIS LICENCE made the date stated in the Particulars hereto BETWEEN the Owner named in the Particulars of the one part and the Timesharer named in the Particulars of the other part WITNESSETH as follows:

[The Grant]

1. In consideration of the Premium specified in the Particulars hereto the Owner HEREBY GRANTS unto the Timesharer a Licence revocable only as hereinafter provided to occupy the Suite specified in the Particulars hereto for the Week or Weeks in each year therein defined until 2025 inclusive TOGETHER with the right to use the Parking Space specified in the Particulars hereto or such alternative parking space as may from time to time be notified to the Timesharer in writing by the Owner

2. The Timesharer may freely assign by way of sale or gift or otherwise the benefit of this Licence for the whole of the Licence Period unexpired at the date of the assignment

3. The Timesharer may authorise and licence other persons to occupy the Suite for holiday purposes only for any Weeks in the Licence Period but the Timesharer shall remain liable for the performance and observance of the covenants herein during the period when any such other persons have been licensed by him to occupy the Suite

4. The Timesharer covenants with the Owner that he will within one calendar month of any assignment or under-letting or devolution of his interest hereunder or (if earlier) before the start of the next Week to which this Licence relates give written notice thereof to the Owner specifying the nature of the event the name and address of the person becoming entitled thereunder to the benefit of the Licence and the Years and Weeks for which they will be so entitled

[The Timesharer's Financial Obligations]

5. (a) The Timesharer HEREBY COVENANTS with the Owner that he will pay to the Owner in each year ending 31st March (hereinafter called 'the financial year') of the Licence Period a Management Charge for each Week to which the Licence relates of the amount specified below

(b) The Management Charge for the financial year ending 31st March 198 will be
For every other financial year the Management Charge will be the amount of the Management Charge for the preceding year plus a further sum proportional to the amount (if any) by which the Retail Price Index for the February next before that year is higher than the Index for the February next before the preceding year

(c) In the event of any change in the reference base used to compile the Index the figure taken to be shown in the Index shall be the figure which would have been shown in it if the reference base current on the date of this Licence had been retained

(d) In the event of it becoming impossible by reason of any change in the method used to compile the Index or for any other reason whatever to calculate the Management Charge by reference to the Retail Price Index then there shall be substituted some other index which in the opinion of the Owner most nearly reflects changes in retail prices and services

(e) The Owner will inform the Timesharer not later than 28 days before the beginning of the financial year of the amount of the Management Charge for the financial year and the Management Charge for the financial year with any Value Added Tax payable thereon shall become due and payable 21 days before the commencement of the first Week in that financial year specified in the Particulars

6. The Timesharer shall not be entitled to go into occupation of the Suite in any financial year unless and until the Management Charge payable by him for that year and any other sums due and owing by him to the Owner under this Licence shall have been paid in full

[The Timesharer's Obligations of Behaviour]

7. The Timesharer HEREBY COVENANTS with the Owner as follows:

(1) Not to take occupation of the Suite before 4 p.m. on the Saturday at the commencement of the Week and to vacate the Suite by 12 noon on the Saturday (or on the last Saturday of any continuous period of more than one Week he is licensed to occupy it)

(2) To keep and maintain the Suite and the contents thereof in a reasonable state and condition and clean and tidy during each Week he occupies it

(3) If required to sign an inventory before going into occupation for any week

(4) To pay the Owner on demand the cost of repairing reinstating or making good any damage caused by him or his family or guests to

the Suite or its contents and of replacing any of the contents lost or damaged by him or them

(5) To notify the Owner of any change in his permanent address

(6) To pay for all electricity consumed in the Suite during his occupation of it

(7) Not to use the Suite or permit or suffer it to be used for any purpose other than as holiday accommodation only

(8) Not to use the Suite or permit or suffer it to be used for any illegal or immoral purpose

(9) Not to allow the Suite to be occupied by more than the number of persons specified in the Particulars hereto as the Permitted Occupancy

(10) Not to do or permit or suffer to be done anything which may be or become a nuisance or annoyance to the Owner or any other Timesharer in the Timeshare Premises or any resident or guest of the Carlton Hotel

(11) Not to do or permit or suffer to be done anything which makes void or voidable or otherwise prejudice any insurance relating to the Suite or its contents or the Timeshare Premises or the contents or increase the premium payable therefore

(12) To observe the Rules from time to time laid down by the Owner and notified to him in writing by the Owner A copy of the Rules currently in force is annexed to this Licence

8. If the Management Charge or any part thereof remains unpaid for three months after becoming due or if there shall be any breach by the Timesharer of his covenants hereunder which shall in the opinion of the Owner be serious and persistent then in any such case the Owner may determine this Licence and thereupon all rights of the Timesharer hereunder shall cease but without prejudice to the Owner's right of action or remedy in respect of any antecedent breach of the Timesharer

9. The Timesharer shall be entitled to use (on the same terms and conditions as the same are available to guests of the Hotel) such facilities as may from time to time be available at the Carlton Hotel

[The Owner's Undertaking]

10. The Owner HEREBY COVENANTS with the Timesharer that subject to payment by the Timesharer of the Management Charge the Owner will:

(1) Maintain repair decorate and renew the main structure exterior and common parts of the Timeshare Premises

(2) Maintain repair and where necessary renew the lifts boilers and installation for central heating and supplying hot water on or serving the Timeshare Premises

(3) Repair and decorate the Suite

(4) Maintain repair and renew when necessary the furniture furnishings fixtures and fittings of the Suite and of the common parts of the Timeshare Premises

(5) Keep clean lighted and heated the common parts of the Timeshare Premises

(6) Maintain the grounds (if any) comprised in the Timeshare Premises

(7) Clean the Suite twice a week

(8) Adequately insure the Timeshare Premises the Suite and the contents of the Suite against such risks including public liability insurance as the Owner considers necessary

(9) To lay out all insurance monies in rebuilding and reinstating the Timeshare Premises or the part thereof destroyed or damaged in accordance with the bye-laws regulations and planning permission of all relevant authorities

(10) To pay all existing and future rates taxes assessments and outgoings now or hereafter imposed or payable in respect of the Timeshare Premises

(11) In the event of the Suite being unavailable in any week from any of the causes specified in clause 11 below for reasonably comfortable occupation by the Timesharer, at the option of the Owner, (a) provide reasonable alternative accommodation for the Timesharer or (b) pay compensation to the Timesharer for each week during which the Suite is unavailable as aforesaid of a sum equal to the weekly letting value of the Suite

11. Save as provided in sub-clause 10(11) above the Owner shall not be under any liability to the Timesharer whether under the covenants on its part herein contained or otherwise in respect of any interruption in the provision of services or any prevention of or interference with the Timesharer's occupation of the Suite caused or arising from fire flood act of God weather conditions war or civil commotion strikes lockouts mechanical breakdown or any other cause beyond the Owner's control

12. The Owner's liability under the covenants herein contained shall cease if the Owner transfers its interest or a lesser interest in the Timeshare Premises to another person who is willing to enter into a covenant with the Timesharer to observe the Owner's covenants under this Licence

13. In this Licence

(1) 'the Owner' shall include the successors in title of the Owner

(2) 'the Timesharer' shall include the successors in title of the Timesharer and all persons claiming through or under him and them

(3) When the Timesharer is more than one person the covenants and obligations on his part herein contained shall be construed as joint and several convenants and obligations

(4) 'the Timesharer Premises' means those parts of the Carlton Hotel in which suites

or rooms are made available by the Owner for timesharing and those parts (if any) of the grounds of the Carlton Hotel which in the opinion of the Owner are ancillary to those parts

[Arbitration]

14. If there shall be any dispute between the Owner and the Timesharer arising out of or relating to this Licence and the provisions hereof the same shall be referred in accordance with the provisions of the Arbitration Acts to a single arbitrator to be appointed in default of agreement by the President for the time being of the Royal Institution of Chartered Surveyors

15. It is hereby certified that the transaction hereby effected does not form part of a larger transaction or series of transactions in respect of which the amount or value or aggregate amount or value of the consideration exceeds £30,000

AS WITNESS the parties have hereunto set their hands the day and year first before written

[Code of Conduct]

THE RULES

FOREWORD

It is not envisaged that the type of client attracted to Carlton Timeshare participation will need to have a code of conduct document but since we are obliged to state the terms and conditions under which licences are granted we have no recourse but to ask you in the interests of all concerned to conform to the rules as follows:

The Licensees shall

(1) Occupy the Suite to which the Licence relates for the appropriate week or weeks and no longer

(2) Not do or permit anything to be done which may in any way constitute or be a nuisance to any other Licensee or any person whatsoever which shall include a prohibition against the washing and drying of clothes anywhere other than in the areas provided for

that purpose and a prohibition against the noisy playing of radios tape recorders television or other instruments in or about the suites of accommodation or elsewhere in such a manner as to constitute a nuisance to neighbouring Licensees

(3) In the event of any emergency repair or maintenance work requiring to be carried out to the suites or their contents during the Licensee's occupancy to allow access to the necessary tradesmen and others to enable such work to be carried out

(4) Be personally liable for the amount of any insurance monies not being recoverable as a result of any action by them which makes void or voidable the insurance to the premises being occupied

(5) Not in any way to make any alterations to the premises to which his Licence relates or the contents thereof

(6) Not bring any animal of any sort into the suites or on to the Timeshare premises

(7) Not park or allow to be parked any vehicle of any sort other than in the designated parking places

SIGNED on behalf of the Owner
by their duly authorised agent
in the presence of

WITNESSED

SIGNED by the Timesharer in the presence of

WITNESSED

11 Club Plan

Whether this be a proprietary club or members club the club rules must not be confused with the comments in the previous chapter. Many locals are attracted to owning at their local resort mainly to make use of its club facilities when they are not in residence. After all, it can cost a lot of money to become family members at good-class country clubs and they often find that their timeshare purchase, which they invariably exchange, gives them the use, year round, of all the amenities.

In the early days this has openly been encouraged by the developers who seek to ensure the all-year-round viability of their health spas, restaurants and sporting facilities building this around local support. The danger here of course is that if you are seeking a quiet relaxing location then country clubs are not for you, since these are often heavily promoted to non-timesharers as social clubs and have local 'outsider' membership in excess of two to three thousand.

Returning, however, to the situation whereby each purchase buys a 'membership' in a club, the membership then entitles the buyer the right to use a specific property for a fixed time period for a specified number of years. In this case the assets of the club are held by a trustee for the sole interest of the club.

Another method is where the purchaser buys 'membership' in a club (not a specific property) which owns or leases a number of properties which members then have the right to use, booking these on a first-cum-first-served basis – rather like a hotel.

The constitution of clubs and their rules need to be

looked at fairly closely since it often reveals that a timesharers' club has two classes of members – founders and ordinary. The founder members are normally the developer and his representatives who form the first committee and lay down the rules. Their election is by the developer's choice and they are exempt from the normal club rules regarding re-election. The very implications of this make the need for caution, before entering a club form of purchase, mandatory.

Slightly more complex are agreements on licences which give you rights as club members and an example is given here of the highly regarded Kilconquhar Castle Club, reproduced unedited with their kind permission. I am sure they will gladly clarify any point that may not be clear.

CONSTITUTION
of
KILCONQUHAR CASTLE CLUB

1. The Club shall be known as "Kilconquhar Castle Club" and shall have its headquarters at Kilconquhar Castle, Kilconquhar, Fife or at such other place as the members shall from time to time determine.

2. The Club shall be an unincorporated association whose members (a) through an independent Trust Corporation (hereinafter referred to as "the Trustee") shall have joint rights of ownership of houses built or to be built at Kilconquhar Castle, Kilconquhar, and (b) personally shall be entitled to occupy one or more of those houses for specific periods during the year.

3. The Founder Member of the Club shall be Kilconquhar Castle Estate Limited a Company incorporated under the Companies Acts, registered in Scotland and having its Registered Office at Kilconquhar Castle, Kilconquhar, Fife.

Understanding the Structure of Timeshare

4. The Founder Member shall at its own expense be responsible for the erection on sites of its choosing at Kilconquhar Castle of houses for occupation by members of the Club and for the furnishing of and provision of services to such houses. Once each house has been completed and furnished the Founder Member shall prepare an Inventory of the house's contents (to be updated and revised by the Committee of the Club as occasion demands) and shall convey the house and its grounds to the Trustee to be held by the Trustee for behoof of the members of the Club.

5. (1) For each house there shall be issued 52 consecutively numbered Holiday Certificates and the holder of a Holiday Certificate shall be entitled to occupy the house to which the Holiday Certificate relates for the period stated on the Holiday Certificate. Each such period shall start on a Saturday at 5 p.m. and end on the following Saturday at 10 a.m. Holiday Certificate Number One shall relate to the period starting at 5 p.m. on the first Saturday each year and so forth weekly thereafter. The exact dates of the periods for the first eighty four years from Seventh January, 1978 shall be as set out in the Table annexed. In every cycle of 28 years there shall be 35 days unallocated to weekly periods, and the right to occupy the houses for such unallocated days shall belong to the Founder Member. Two of said Holiday Certificates for each house shall not be specifically allocated but shall belong to Kilconquhar Castle Club to enable necessary maintenance and repairs to be carried out each year during the period to which said two Holiday Certificates relate; no management charges shall be payable in respect of

the said two Holiday Certificates. The Founder Member shall initially be entitled to the remaining fifty Holiday Certificates in respect of each house conveyed to the Trustee.

(2) Notwithstanding the terms of subsection (1) of this Article
(a) It shall be competent to issue Holiday Certificates for "Christmas Period" and "New Year Period" such periods to commence on 23rd December and 30th December respectively at 5 p.m. and to end on 30th December and 6 January respectively at 10 a.m. every year. For each house where Holiday Certificates are issued for such periods Holiday Certificates for periods Numbers One, Fifty, Fifty one, and Fifty two (or One A, Fifty A, Fifty one A and Fifty two A as the case may be) shall not be issued. Any unallocated days shall initially belong to the Founder Member.
(b) It shall be competent to issue Holiday Certificates for periods to commence twenty four hours earlier than stated in subsection (1) of this Article: the number of any Holiday Certificates so issued shall bear the suffix "A".

6. Any person shall be entitled to apply for and be admitted to membership of the Club. Both the Founder Member and the Committee shall have power to admit applicants to membership. Upon being admitted to membership the new members shall be bound to take up at least one Holiday Certificate. The membership of any person who for a consecutive period of 14 days does not hold a Holiday Certificate shall lapse and that person shall on the expiry of the 14th day cease to be a member of the Club. For the purposes of this Article "person" shall

Understanding the Structure of Timeshare

include partnership, unincorporated association and incorporated company.

7. (1) Holiday Certificates shall be purchased or otherwise acquired from existing or retiring members including the Founder Member or the representatives of deceased members. All transfers shall be in a form to be approved by the Founder Member and the Committee and shall be registered with the Committee which shall maintain a Register of Holiday Certificates which shall include information showing the name and address of the current holder of each Certificate. No right to a Holiday Certificate shall be effective until so registered. The Committee shall not register any transfer until all charges and liabilities due by the existing holder to the Club have been settled in full.

   (2) Notwithstanding the foregoing in the event of the Committee receiving intimation from a lender of the granting of an assignation in security by a member of that member's interest in a Holiday Certificate the Committee shall amend the Register of Holiday Certificates to show the name of the party in whose name the assignation in security has been granted as the Holder of the Holiday Certificate. However, it is understood that despite the registration of the party in whose favour the assignation in security has been granted as the party entitled to the Holiday Certificate, that party shall not be obliged to comply with the obligations of a Certificate Holder under this Constitution which shall still be imposed on the party granting the assignation in security.

8. The management of the Club's property and affairs shall be vested in a Committee of 5

persons, two of whom shall be nominated by the Founder Member (and need not be members of the Club) and the remainder of whom shall be members of the Club elected by the members in General Meeting. The first three elected members of the Committee shall be elected at the first General Meeting of the Club which shall be held within twelve months of the first house being completed and conveyed to the Trustee in terms of Article 4 hereof. The first General Meeting shall be convened by the Founder Member who shall give not less than 14 days' notice in writing to every member of the meeting. At each Annual General Meeting of the Club, one elected member shall retire and a new member shall be elected. The order in which the first three members shall retire shall be determined by the drawing of lots and thereafter retirals shall be by rotation, each member retiring after three years. Retiring members shall be eligible for re-election.

(2) The members of the Club in General Meeting shall elect three alternate members of the Committee. In the event of an elected Member of Committee being unable to attend a meeting of the Committee he shall invite the first alternate member of Committee to attend and vote at such meeting in his stead. If the first alternate is unable to attend the second alternate shall be so invited and if he is also unable to attend the third alternate shall be so invited.

(3) In the event of there being a ballot for election of members or alternate members of Committee any vacancy or vacancies on the Committee shall be filled by the Candidate or Candidates securing the highest number of votes cast and the candidates receiving the next highest number of votes cast shall

Understanding the Structure of Timeshare

be deemed to be elected as the first, second and third alternate members of the Committee. In the event of there being no ballot the order of the alternate members of Committee shall be decided by lot. Alternate members of Committee shall serve for one year only but shall be eligible for re-election.

9. The Committee shall meet as often as shall be necessary for the proper management of the affairs of the Club. The Committee shall ordinarily at each meeting fix the date, time and place of its next meeting, but in addition, any two Committee members shall be entitled to call a Committee Meeting by giving not less than 7 days' notice in writing to all members of the Committee. Decisions of the Committee shall be determined by a majority of the Committee members present and voting. All decisions of the Committee shall be recorded in a Minute Book which shall be open to inspection by all members of the Club at the Club's headquarters.

10. The Chairman of the Committee shall be nominated by the Founder Member and shall have a casting vote at Committee meetings in the event of the votes being equally divided. In the absence of the Chairman so nominated by the Founder Member the other Committee Member nominated by the Founder Member shall be the Chairman of the Meeting and shall likewise have a casting vote in the event of the votes being equally divided. In the absence of both Committee Members nominated by the Founder Member the elected Committee Members shall by majority vote elect a Chairman for the meeting from their own number who shall have a casting vote in the event of the votes being equally divided.

11. Three members of the Committee shall constitute a quorum at Committee meetings.

12. The Committee shall have full power to do all things that may be necessary for the carrying out of the objects of the Club and for its general management. Until such time as the Committee shall have been constituted the Founder Member shall be responsible for fulfilling the functions of the Committee.

13. The Committee shall be obliged:–
(a) to keep proper books of account and to have the same audited by a Chartered Accountant each year and presented to the Club. Such Chartered Accountant shall initially be appointed by the Founder Member, but thereafter at the First General Meeting of the Club and at the Annual General Meeting of the Club in each year thereafter shall be appointed by the Club in General Meeting.
(b) to co-opt a member of the Club to fill any casual vacancy on the Committee caused by the death, incapacity or resignation of any of the elected members of Committee at the first Committee meeting following such death, incapacity or resignation. All such persons so appointed shall hold office only until the immediately following Annual General Meeting but shall be eligible for election for the unexpired portion of the term of office of the Committee member in whose stead they were co-opted.
(c) to make such bye-laws as may be necessary for the proper regulation of the Club and its affairs. Such bye-laws shall be valid and binding on all members of the Club unless and until either revoked by the Committee or set aside by the members of the Club in General Meeting.
(d) to cancel or suspend the membership of any

Understanding the Structure of Timeshare

member who shall at any time be shown to the satisfaction of the Committee to have committed a breach of the rules or bye-laws of the club or to have conducted himself or herself in a manner unbecoming to a member of the Club. The decision of the Committee shall be final, but it shall have due regard to the principles of natural justice.

(e) to appoint such professional advisers as may be necessary.

(f) in the event of the Trustee resigning or going into liquidation to appoint another Trust Corporation as Trustee of the Club's heritable property and to instruct the conveyance of the Club's heritable property to such new Trustee.

13A In the event of any Member being expelled from Membership of the Club and failing to dispose of his or her Holiday Certificate or Certificates the following provisions shall apply:

(a) The Committee shall on behalf of Kilconquhar Castle Club after six months from the date of such expulsion be empowered and after twelve months from the date of such expulsion be obliged to require such expelled Member to sell to the committee on behalf of the Club any Holiday Certificate or Certificates still registered in the name of such expelled Member at the price or prices paid by such expelled Member for such Holiday Certificate or Certificates.

(b) In the event of any of such Holiday Certificates having been acquired by such expelled Member other than by Purchase, the price payable by the Committee to the expelled Member shall be the most recent price paid for such Holiday Certificate.

(c) The Committee shall deduct from the price

payable (i) any outstanding management charges or proportion of costs due under Article 16 of the Constitution of the Club and (ii) any sums due in terms of Article 17 (b) or (d) of the Constitution of the Club.

(d) Notice in writing of the exercise of such power or of the implementation of such obligation shall be given in writing to such expelled Member by recorded delivery letter sent to such expelled Member's last known address together with a cheque for the total sum payable.

(e) The Committee shall be empowered to execute on behalf of such expelled Member any forms of transfer of Holiday Certificate necessary to implement its powers and obligations under this Article.

14. Any vacancies on the Committee caused by the death, incapacity or resignation of any of the nominees of the Founder Member shall be filled by a new nominee of the Founder Member.

15. The Committee shall be entitled to delegate such of its functions as shall to it seem proper to a sub-committee or committees or to a Management Company on such terms and conditions as shall be agreed between the Committee and the Management Company, including terms and conditions governing the remuneration of the Management Company. The Founder Member and members of the Club shall not be precluded from being the Management Company.

16. The members of the club shall contribute, in proportion to the number of Holiday Certificates held by them to the whole costs incurred by the Club, including without prejudice to the foregoing generality the cost of the following:–

(a) Maintenance, repair, redecoration (where appropriate) cleansing, and when necessary renewal of the structure, exterior and interior of the house, and the whole services, roadways, and amenity area, whether exclusive, common, mutual or otherwise.
(b) Maintenance, repair and when necessary replacement of the whole furniture, furnishings, plenishings, fittings and fixtures in, on, about or pertaining to the houses.
(c) Insurance of the Club's property both heritable and moveable for the full reinstatement value thereof and any other insurances which the Committee shall consider necessary and appropriate.
(d) The whole outgoing incurred in respect of the Club's property including rates, feuduties, and other charges or impositions, whether of an annual or recurring nature or otherwise.
(e) The routine maintenance, cleaning and tidying of the interior and exterior of the houses and the amenity ground and other pertaining thereto.
(f) All works and others which are required to be done to comply with any statutory provisions or the directions or notices of any Governmental, Local or Public Authority.
(g) Any factorial and management charges or any other charges whatsoever which may be incurred in the management of the Club's property and the running of the Club's affairs including the fees and expenses of the Trustee.

Except insofar as the same may have been delegated to the Management Company hereinbefore referred to, the Committee shall have sole discretion in deciding what monies should be spent for any of the foregoing purposes and when the same should be spent. The Committee shall also have discretion to fix what proportion of the total cost expended shall be borne by the holders of different Holiday Certificates in respect that the Holiday Certificates may be for different types of houses.

The club shall have power:–

(a) to borrow money.
(b) to grant securities over its property.
(c) to purchase, lease or otherwise acquire additional property and,
    (d) to sell, feu, lease, grant servitudes and wayleaves over, or otherwise dispose of its property or any rights over its property.

    but the foregoing powers shall be exerciseable only upon a decision by a three-quarters majority of votes cast at a General meeting.

17. The following obligations shall rest with each of the holders of the Holiday Certificates:

(a) Not to occupy the premises to which his or her Holiday Certificate relates for any longer than the appropriate period of time in each year. The premises shall not be used for any trade, occupation, business or commerce and there shall be a strict prohibition on the doing of anything which shall in any way constitute or be a nuisance to any other members of the Club or any other person whatsoever, which shall include a prohibition against the drying of clothes and washing anywhere other than in the drying room provided for that purpose and a prohibition against the noisy playing of radios, tape recorders, or other instruments in such a way as to constitute a nuisance to neighbouring members. The ground belonging to the Club so far as unbuilt on

shall be used as amenity ground only.
(b) To keep and maintain the premises (both structure and contents) to which his or her Certificate relates in a reasonable state and condition during the period of his or her occupancy, the Certificate holder being personally liable for any damage, deterioration or dilapidation over and above fair wear and tear which may have taken place during his or her period of occupation, as to which the Committee, or in the event of a Management Company having been appointed as aforesaid, the Management Company shall be the sole judge.
(c) in the event of any repair or maintenance work requiring to be carried out to the house or its contents during the period of a Certificate holder's occupancy of the house, to allow access to the necessary tradesmen and others to enable such work to be carried out.
(d) Not to do anything which would make void or voidable the insurance of the premises and contents being occupied. In the event of the Certificate holder so doing and any insurance monies not being recoverable as a result the Certificate holder shall be personally liable for the amount so irrecoverable.
(e) Not in any way to make any alterations to the premises to which his or her Certificate relates or the contents thereof.
(f) To pay within one month of its being demanded the annual management charge being either the appropriate proportion of all the costs incurred by the Club in terms of Article 16 hereof or the management charge payable to the Management Company in the event of a Management Company having been appointed as hereinbefore provided; and to pay also any charge falling due under Paragraphs (b) and (d) of this Article. In the event of any of the said sums not being paid

by the due date the Committee or the Management Company as the case may be shall be entitled to refuse the holder in question occupation of the house to which his or her Certificate relates until all arrears have been settled.

(g) To pay for all electricity consumed by him or her in the house which he or she is occupying.

(h) To notify the Committee or in the event of a Management Company having been appointed as hereinbefore provided, the Management Company, forthwith of any change of his or her permanent address.

(i) In the event of his or her transferring his or her Certificate upon a sale thereof or otherwise, or letting or for any reason otherwise parting with possession of the premises to which his or her Certificate relates for a part or the whole of the period to which his or her Certificate relates, immediately to intimate the same to the Committee or the Management Company in the event of a Management Company having been appointed as hereinbefore provided, together with notification of the name and address of the person to whom he or she has transferred his or her Certificate or ceded his or her possession.

18. A member shall be entitled to let the premises to which his or her Certificate relates for the whole or part of the period to which his or her Certificate relates, subject to notification being given in terms of Article 17 (i) hereof, but the member shall during the period of such let remain the holder of the Certificate and shall be primarily responsible for all obligations incumbent on the holder of the Certificate.

19. The Annual General Meeting of the Club shall be held at Kilconquhar Castle, Kil-

Understanding the Structure of Timeshare 73

conquhar, or such other place as the Committee shall decide on such date as the Committee may decide in each year. It shall be called by giving not less than 21 days' notice in writing sent to all members with the Agenda of the business to be conducted at such meeting.

20. The Committee shall be entitled, of its own resolve, or shall be bound upon a request in writing from either (a) the Founder Member or (b) the holders of not less than 50% of the Holiday Certificates not held by the Founder Member to call a Special General Meeting of the club and such meeting shall be called in the manner prescribed for an Annual General Meeting save that 14 days' notice only shall be necessary.

21. At every General Meeting the Chairman of the Committee whom failing a Chairman appointed by a majority vote of the members present at the meeting shall preside. Each member shall be entitled to one vote for each Holiday Certificate held. Members will be entitled to appoint proxies to vote in their stead provided intimation in writing is given to the Committee at least 7 days prior to the meeting. At all meetings in the case of an equality of votes the Chairman shall have a casting vote. In the case of a Special General Meeting no business other than that specifically stated in the notice calling the meeting shall be considered. Any resolution to be proposed otherwise than by the Committee at any General Meeting of the Club shall be intimated in writing to the Committee not less than 14 days before the date of the meeting if it is an Annual General Meeting or 7 days if it is a Special General Meeting and shall be signed by the proposer and seconder.

22. In the event of the assets of the Club for any reason being distributed amongst the members of the Club the same shall be distributed in accordance with the relative values of the Holiday Certificates held by the members as determined by a valuer to be appointed by the President of The Royal Institute of Chartered Surveyors.

23. Nothing in this Constitution shall prevent either a member whose membership has been suspended or a former member whose membership has been cancelled from disposing in whatever way he or she sees fit of any Holiday Certificates registered in his or her name, subject always to the provision of Article 13A or Article 7 hereof.

24. The Constitution of the Club shall not be alterable except at a General Meeting of the Club and then only if
(a) At least 10 days' notice in writing shall have been given to all Members of the Club including the Founder Member of any proposed alterations to the Constitution and
(b) The proposed alterations are approved at such General Meeting by the Founder Member and the holders of at least two thirds of the Holiday Certificates not held by the Founder Member present and voting
A resolution proposing alterations to the Constitution of the Club shall not be considered unless it has been submitted in writing by either the Committee or the Founder Member or any other 10 Members of the Club.

25. Any dispute or difference arising out of these presents shall be referred to the decision of a single expert, to be agreed between the parties or in default of

agreement to be appointed on the application of either party by the President for the time being of the Law Society of Scotland, to act as an expert and not an arbiter.

12 Legal Procedures (When to Take Advice)

Some people become confused when they consider the legalities of purchasing a timeshare property and this stems largely from the fact that they are conditioned to the more established procedures one must follow when buying a house or apartment in the normal way. Each country of course will differ in terms of the rules to be observed but in the general sense, where you are buying a licence giving you the right to use something, you will find that the steps are very simple and whatever legal costs are involved are usually absorbed by the developer.

The whole process is set in motion by a viewing of the product on offer and this in most cases is on site. Should the prospective timesharers be sufficiently motivated to take it to the next stage, they will be invited to complete a simple reservation form which has generally no legal significance and is merely an undertaking by the developer to hold that week or weeks for a period of ten days.

This is accompanied by a 10 per cent deposit which (unless cash) is not banked for the same period. Usually it is banked only when the timesharer gives the go ahead and then normally together with the balance at the time of completion.

At this point the timesharer can expect to receive a copy of the licence (see sample, in Chapter 10) and is recommended to seek the advice of his or her solicitor on its content. Assuming that the advice received favours proceeding to completion, the timesharer advises the developer or his agent and a further two original copies of the licence are forwarded.

It is a matter of conjecture at this point whether or not the deposit should be banked but most developers would probably agree that it is more convenient to bank both cheques together since if at a later stage the deal falls through it is a nuisance having to raise cheques in refund.

The signed copy of the licence to be retained by the timesharer will have appended as a rule a copy of the timeshare calender and an inventory of the suite contents. It would be as well for timesharers to ask for this if it is not sent since they will usually be responsible for reporting any discrepancies each time they visit. Failure to do so might result in their facing charges related to any missing or broken items.

Some developments actually do charge a deposit (particularly to exchangees) which is fully refundable if all is in order when they leave.

Naturally we have all learned to be wary of anything that appears over-simple and it should always be uppermost in your mind that before you sign anything you will go and have a chat with your solicitor even though the developer's representative assures you that it is not necessary.

In truth this may well be right since some timeshare resorts can boast a large number of solicitors amongst their customers, none of whom would have bought unless they were totally satisfied about their rights. Even so, at the end of the day you will only have peace of mind if you take this step and there is less danger in your having overlooked seemingly insignificant clauses which might prove vital in the event of a dispute.

Perhaps the least complicated procedure is the purchase of a right to use licence for a given term of say forty or eighty years in England or Wales and a typical agreement is given as an example in Chapter 10, pp. 51-8. The rights of both parties are set out very clearly and even the least legal-minded among us should have no difficult in understanding it.

Where it is open to interpretation then your solicitor will have no hesitation in pointing this out and seeking clarification on your behalf if needed. With the popularity of timeshare in recent years there is a good chance that your solicitor will have had exposure to similar agreements and he or she will know instinctively what to look for.

Of course there are some solicitors, who for reasons of their own, have set their minds against timeshare and you must be prepared to accept that you may have a hard choice to make if your instincts tell you it is right for you and your solicitor adopts an opposite view.

It is a known fact that most of us go to our solicitors to have them confirm what *we* think and it is sometimes unpalatable to receive a contrary viewpoint. Equally it must be said that solicitors, if consulted, will feel obliged to give an opinion and that opinion can only be based on the facts laid before them.

They will not have been able to see the resort as you have or form opinions on the people you have met in whom you will be placing your trust. They have learned to be cautious and even sceptical about these matters so do not expect to be greeted by the same enthusiasm for the product that you feel and try not to feel hurt or irritated when they appear to be throwing cold water on the project.

Not quite so simple but still not too complicated is the purchase of a right to use licence for life which is only available within the UK in Scotland. We often hear the expression 'Scotland is different' and it is true to say that its judicial system is indeed very different.

In England and Wales the anti-perpetuity laws prevent you from purchasing property of this nature for life, and indeed eighty years is the maximum. But in Scotland no such laws apply and you can and will be able to buy in perpetuity.

Again your developer will offer to guide your steps but if you are not happy about this then you would be advised to ask a Scottish-based solicitor to look at the agreement. Many practices in England and Wales either have branches or associate companies in Scotland so it need not be a problem.

The administration in each development will vary with the needs of the timesharer and the availability of amenities or services but it can be safely assumed that some four weeks before occupancy they will be invited to complete a form stating basics like number of people coming, bedding requirements, grocery provisions needed, together with any special requests for bookings in the restaurants, at the hairdressers, car hire, taxis at the airport or station, teeing off times at local golf courses and for any other services within the scope of the developer to supply.

Most developers are able to provide a guaranteed car parking space during the timesharer's period of occupancy but this should not be taken for granted and the developer will appreciate knowing in advance your car registration number so that those detailed to police the area will spot any interlopers at once. This is not vital so far in advance but it should not be overlooked when checking in.

Some developers are known to seek deposits by way of a credit card imprint, gladly accepting the small percentage loss of margin in order to make the transaction secure – the reasoning being that cheques are too easily cancelled. If you encounter this ploy then your instinct should tell you to beware.

Naturally these forms of purchase grow in complexity when you buy overseas and on these occasions it is vital to use the service of a recommended local solicitor or one in the UK with strong affiliations in the country of purchase. You will probably be assured that this is not necessary and that you are incurring unwarranted expense.

You may even be given examples of typical expenditure to put you off, and you will have to reconcile such examples with developers' assurances that 'all legal fees are taken care of' which you will have heard earlier in the presentation. Can it really be that they can be played down one moment and escalated so horrifically the next when you show an interest in checking direct.

Of course using an overseas solicitor independently can be expensive and protracted. Legal costs are built into the selling price already and you may be spending more than you need to, but it might be money well spent in the long run.

If you accept that at the outset the developer will have taken all of his overheads and related costs in the creation of the project into account and that these will have been absorbed within the selling price, then you can expect your own solicitor to charge according to the amount of time spent on giving you advice.

It might be as little as £35 within the UK but of course it can be considerably more if letters are written on your behalf or correspondence entered into with a third party.

For advice taken abroad you can expect somewhat higher charges and a friend of mine recently paid 74,000 pesetas (approximately £360) to a Spanish solicitor for a relatively simple clearance of a technical point related to house purchase. Generally though something under £100 would be the norm, but do find out the costs in advance if you can.

Some projects, after all, are offered on a relatively short term (twenty-five years) licence with the proposal that it be sold after this time and the proceeds equally divided – after costs. You can imagine how complicated that can become in a foreign language and clearly is one instance when you need to have a qualified mind focused on the proposition.

And of course 'in perpetuity' can mean in your lifetime only by a subtle play on words which is not crystal clear even to those who speak the language fluently. Your rights under club membership too can rotate through a wide spectrum in foreign 'legalese' so it really does become necessary to take expert advice if you want to sleep nights.

One point that always seems to worry potential timesharers is the question of what happens to their timeshare when the right to use licence period expires. The answer is simple – it reverts to the developer since what the timesharer has bought is the right to use for the forty years or so offered and the price paid reflects the projected, commercial value of those forty weeks (assuming it was only one week purchased).

It is conceivable that during this time the developer may decide to give the timesharer an option to extend the period of the licence and the cost of this will again reflect the projected value. There is however no obligation on the

Understanding the Structure of Timeshare

part of the developer to make such an offer and some timesharers find difficulty in accepting this.

Some hotel developers, for example, adopt timeshare as a means of modernizing a section of their hotels and this is financed by the timesharer who enjoys access for the agreed period. At the end of this time the suites will be released for hotel use once more, and everyone should be happy about the arrangement.

It is a feature of timeshare however that the timesharers become possessive (after all, in their eyes at least they are 'owners') about their purchase and do not contemplate with relish or enthusiasm the termination of their agreements. Perhaps this in itself is a measure of satisfaction with their purchase.

To summarize then: you are likely to have received various documents, the number and complexity of which will depend largely on the scale of administrative detail provided by the development into which you are purchasing. You should, however, be given:

1. A receipt for your deposit – usually a reservation form.
2. A calendar of the weeks and when they occur.
3. An inventory of the suite/apartment/villa contents.
4. A plan of the building in which your unit is located.
5. A layout plan for your unit.
6. A brochure describing what you are purchasing – very important if you wish to contest the terms under which you purchased at some later date.
7. A signed and witnessed copy of the licence (take a photocopy as soon as you receive it as so many people seem to misplace them).

There will in all probably be some correspondence and you should file this with all relevant documentation where it can easily be located at some future point.

Timeshare Calendar

The following represents a typical timeshare calendar and shows the first twenty years only. The full term in this instance takes us to the year 2025 but others span an eighty-year period.

ALWAYS 29 DEC – 5 JAN

WEEK NUMBERS

Year	1	2	M	3	4	5	6	7	8	9	10	11	12	13	14	15	16	17	18	19	20	21	22	23	24	25	26
1982		5/1	M	16/1	23/1	30/1	6/2	13/2	20/2	27/2	6/3	13/3	20/3	27/3	3/4	10/4	17/4	24/4	1/5	8/5	15/5	22/5	29/5	5/6	12/6	19/6	26/6
1983		5/1	M	15/1	22/1	29/1	5/2	12/2	19/2	26/2	5/3	12/3	19/3	26/3	2/4	9/4	16/4	23/4	30/4	7/5	14/5	21/5	28/5	4/6	11/6	18/6	25/6
1984		5/1	M	14/1	21/1	28/1	4/2	11/2	18/2	25/2	3/3	10/3	17/3	24/3	31/3	7/4	14/4	21/4	28/4	5/5	12/5	19/5	26/5	2/6	9/6	16/6	23/6
1985		5/1	M	12/1	19/1	26/1	2/2	9/2	16/2	23/2	2/3	9/3	16/3	23/3	30/3	6/4	13/4	20/4	27/4	4/5	11/5	18/5	25/5	1/6	8/6	15/6	22/6
1986		5/1	M	18/1	25/1	1/2	8/2	15/2	22/2	1/3	8/3	15/3	22/3	29/3	5/4	12/4	19/4	26/4	3/5	10/5	17/5	24/5	31/5	7/6	14/6	21/6	28/8
1987		5/1	M	17/1	24/1	31/1	7/2	14/2	21/2	28/2	7/3	14/3	21/3	28/3	4/4	11/4	18/4	25/4	2/5	9/5	16/5	23/5	30/5	6/6	13/6	20/6	27/6
1988		5/1	M	16/1	23/1	30/1	6/2	13/2	20/2	27/2	5/3	12/3	19/3	26/3	2/4	9/4	16/4	23/4	30/4	7/5	14/5	21/5	28/5	4/6	11/6	18/6	25/6
1989		5/1	M	14/1	21/1	28/1	4/2	11/2	18/2	25/2	4/3	11/3	18/3	25/3	1/4	8/4	15/4	22/4	29/4	6/5	13/5	20/5	27/5	3/6	10/6	17/6	25/6
1990		5/1	M	13/1	20/1	27/1	3/2	10/2	17/2	24/2	3/3	10/3	17/3	24/3	31/3	7/4	14/4	21/4	28/4	5/5	12/5	19/5	26/5	2/6	9/6	16/6	25/6
1991		5/1	M	12/1	19/1	26/1	2/2	9/2	16/2	23/2	2/3	9/3	16/3	23/3	30/3	6/4	13/4	20/4	27/4	4/5	11/5	18/5	25/5	1/6	8/6	15/6	24/6
1992		5/1	M	18/1	25/1	1/2	8/2	15/2	22/2	29/2	7/3	14/3	21/3	28/3	4/4	11/4	18/4	25/4	2/5	9/5	16/5	23/5	30/5	6/6	13/6	20/6	23/6
1993		5/1	M	16/1	23/1	30/1	6/2	13/2	20/2	27/2	6/3	13/3	20/3	27/3	3/4	10/4	17/4	24/4	1/5	8/5	15/5	22/5	29/5	5/6	12/6	19/6	22/6
1994		5/1	M	15/1	22/1	29/1	5/2	12/2	19/2	26/2	5/3	12/3	19/3	26/3	2/4	9/4	16/4	23/4	30/4	7/5	14/5	21/5	28/5	4/6	11/6	18/6	22/6
1995		5/1	M	14/1	21/1	28/1	4/2	11/2	18/2	25/2	4/3	11/3	18/3	25/3	1/4	8/4	15/4	22/4	29/4	6/5	13/5	20/5	27/5	3/6	10/6	17/6	27/6
1996		5/1	M	13/1	20/1	27/1	3/2	10/2	17/2	24/2	2/3	9/3	16/3	23/3	30/3	6/4	13/4	20/4	27/4	4/5	11/5	18/5	25/5	1/6	8/6	15/6	26/6
1997		5/1	M	18/1	25/1	1/2	8/2	15/2	22/2	1/3	8/3	15/3	22/3	29/3	5/4	12/4	19/4	26/4	3/5	10/5	17/5	24/5	31/5	7/6	14/6	22/6	28/6
1998		5/1	M	17/1	24/1	31/1	7/2	14/2	21/2	28/2	7/3	14/3	21/3	28/3	4/4	11/4	18/4	25/4	2/5	9/5	16/5	23/5	30/5	6/6	13/6	20/6	27/6
1999		5/1	M	16/1	23/1	30/1	6/2	13/2	20/2	27/2	6/3	13/3	20/3	27/3	3/4	10/4	17/4	24/4	1/5	8/5	15/5	22/5	29/5	5/6	12/6	19/6	26/6
2000		5/1	M	15/1	22/1	29/1	5/2	12/2	19/2	26/2	4/3	11/3	18/3	25/3	1/4	8/4	15/4	22/4	29/4	6/5	13/5	20/5	27/5	3/6	10/6	17/6	24/6
2001		5/1	M	13/1	20/1	27/1	3/2	10/2	17/2	24/2	3/3	10/3	17/3	24/3	31/3	7/4	14/4	21/4	28/4	5/5	12/5	19/5	26/5	2/6	9/6	16/6	23/6
2002		5/1	M	12/1	19/1	26/1	2/2	9/2	16/2	23/2	2/3	9/3	16/3	23/3	30/3	6/4	13/4	20/4	27/4	4/5	11/5	18/5	25/5	1/6	8/6	15/6	22/6

ALWAYS 22 DEC – 29 DEC

27	28	29	30	31	32	33	34	35	36	37	38	39	40	41	42	43	44	45	46	47	48	49	M	51	52
3/7	10/7	17/7	24/7	31/7	7/8	14/8	21/8	28/8	4/9	11/9	18/9	25/9	2/10	9/10	16/10	23/10	30/10	6/11	13/11	20/11	27/11	4/12	M	15/12	
2/7	9/7	16/7	23/7	30/7	6/8	13/8	20/8	27/8	3/9	10/9	17/9	24/9	1/10	8/10	15/10	22/10	29/10	5/11	12/11	19/11	26/11	3/12	M	15/12	
30/6	7/7	14/7	21/7	28/7	4/8	11/8	18/8	25/8	1/9	8/9	15/9	22/9	29/9	6/10	13/10	20/10	27/10	3/11	10/11	17/11	24/11	1/12	M	15/12	
29/6	6/7	13/7	20/7	27/7	3/8	10/8	17/8	24/8	31/8	7/9	14/9	21/9	28/9	5/10	12/10	19/10	26/10	2/11	9/11	16/11	23/11	30/11	M	15/12	
5/7	12/7	19/7	26/7	2/8	9/8	16/8	23/8	30/8	6/9	13/9	20/9	27/9	4/10	11/10	18/10	25/10	1/11	8/11	15/11	22/11	29/11	6/12	M	15/12	
4/7	11/7	18/7	25/7	1/8	8/8	15/8	22/8	29/8	5/9	12/9	19/9	26/9	3/10	10/10	17/10	24/10	31/10	7/11	14/11	21/11	28/11	5/12	M	15/12	
2/7	9/7	16/7	23/7	30/7	6/8	13/8	20/8	27/8	3/9	10/9	17/9	24/9	1/10	8/10	15/10	22/10	29/10	5/11	12/11	19/11	26/11	3/12	M	15/12	
1/7	8/7	15/7	22/7	29/7	5/8	12/8	19/8	26/8	2/9	9/9	16/9	23/9	30/9	7/10	14/10	21/10	28/10	4/11	11/11	18/11	25/11	2/12	M	15/12	
30/6	7/7	14/7	21/7	28/7	4/8	11/8	18/8	25/8	1/9	8/9	15/9	22/9	29/9	6/10	13/10	20/10	27/10	3/11	10/11	17/11	24/11	1/12	M	15/12	
29/6	6/7	13/7	20/7	27/7	3/8	10/8	17/8	24/8	31/8	7/9	14/9	21/9	28/9	5/10	12/10	19/10	26/10	2/11	9/11	16/11	23/11	30/11	M	15/12	
4/7	11/7	18/7	25/7	1/8	8/8	15/8	22/8	29/8	5/9	12/9	19/9	26/9	3/10	10/10	17/10	24/10	31/10	7/11	14/11	21/11	28/11	5/12	M	15/12	
3/7	10/7	17/7	24/7	31/7	7/8	14/8	21/8	28/8	4/9	11/9	18/9	25/9	2/10	9/10	16/10	23/10	30/10	6/11	13/11	20/11	27/11	4/12	M	15/12	
2/7	9/7	16/7	23/7	30/7	6/8	13/8	20/8	27/8	3/9	10/9	17/9	24/9	1/10	8/10	15/10	22/10	29/10	5/11	12/11	19/11	26/11	3/12	M	15/12	
1/7	8/7	15/7	22/7	29/7	5/8	12/8	19/8	26/8	2/9	9/9	16/9	23/9	30/9	7/10	14/10	21/10	28/10	4/11	11/11	18/11	25/11	2/12	M	15/12	
29/6	6/7	13/7	20/7	27/7	3/8	10/8	17/8	24/8	31/8	7/9	14/9	21/9	28/9	5/10	12/10	19/10	26/10	2/11	9/11	16/11	23/11	30/11	M	15/12	
5/7	12/7	19/7	26/7	2/8	9/8	16/8	23/8	30/8	6/9	13/9	20/9	27/9	4/10	11/10	18/10	25/10	1/11	8/11	15/11	22/11	29/11	6/12	M	15/12	
4/7	11/7	18/7	25/7	1/8	8/8	15/8	22/8	29/8	5/9	12/9	19/9	26/9	3/10	10/10	17/10	24/10	31/10	7/11	14/11	21/11	28/11	5/12	M	15/12	
3/7	10/7	17/7	24/7	31/7	7/8	14/8	21/8	28/8	4/9	11/9	18/9	25/9	2/10	9/10	16/10	23/10	30/10	6/11	13/11	20/11	27/11	4/12	M	15/12	
1/7	8/7	15/7	22/7	29/7	5/8	12/8	19/8	26/8	2/9	9/9	16/9	23/9	30/9	7/10	14/10	21/10	28/10	4/11	11/11	18/11	25/11	2/12	M	15/12	
30/6	7/7	14/7	21/7	28/7	4/8	11/8	18/8	25/8	1/9	8/9	15/9	22/9	29/9	6/10	13/10	20/10	27/10	3/11	10/11	17/11	24/11	1/12	M	15/12	
29/6	6/7	13/7	20/7	27/7	3/8	10/8	17/8	24/8	31/8	7/9	14/9	21/9	28/9	5/10	12/10	19/10	26/10	2/11	9/11	16/11	23/11	30/11	M	15/12	

The years are divided into 51 weekly (7 night) periods, 47 starting and finishing on a Saturday and 4 starting and finishing on a fixed date. This arrangement provides two separate consecutive weeks covering the Christmas and New Year period; Christmas week (52) begins on 22 December and New Year week (1) on 29 December with occupancy until the mornings of 29 December and 5 January respectively.

Week numbers 3 to 49 begin on Saturdays with occupancy until the following Saturday morning. The unallocated days between weeks 2 and 3 and weeks 49 and 51 will be used for maintenance purposes.

The weeks which include public holidays in England are shown by printing in bold for New Year's Day (week 1); Good Friday and Easter Monday which are in consecutive weeks; and Christmas Day and Boxing Day which both fall in week 52. The weeks printed in italic include the May Day, Spring and Late Summer Bank Holiday Mondays.

13 Disposal

How Do I Dispose of My Timeshare if I Need to Sell?

Most people embark on a timeshare purchase with a view to many years of happy ownership but fate tends to create ever-changing circumstances. (There is nothing more certain than change.) Bereavements, overseas appointments, redundancies, ill-health, divorce – they all play their part in making it necessary for timesharers to dispose of their property and there are a variety of methods open to them in this connection.

The first and obvious choice is the developer who sold it to them initially. He will, for a fee ranging from ten to twenty per cent, offer the week(s) alongside his own unsold weeks to enquirers and how successful he is will largely depend on the commission arrangements with his sales people.

The nature of the beast is such that his sales force might well be receiving high commissions on new properties sold but next to nothing (or even nothing at all) on resales. In these circumstances the resale will take a very long time through this outlet, unless of course the project is nearing a sell-out and weeks are very scarce.

The next choice timesharers have is that they can sell direct, generally without any restraint, thus saving the commission. To do this they can place advertisements in the property section of their local newspaper or in the columns of the national papers – the latter is more expensive, of course, but does reach a much wider audience.

An advertisement in one of the specialist journals such

as *Homes Abroad* can also be very effective.

Timesharers have reported varying degrees of success from direct advertising but the savings on commission if they do sell is still a powerful incentive.

There are now also a number of specialist companies emerging which handle timeshare resales and prominent amongst these is the Timeshare Bourse which is operated by the Tourism Advisory Group Ltd who claim to be Europe's largest rental and resale organization in the timeshare industry.

Working, as the name suggests, like an international stock exchange, buyers and sellers are brought together via Prestel, used extensively by a network of specialist brokers and agents.

A listing for an existing private owner is currently £39.50 refundable upon sale completion and there is a 17½ per cent commission chargeable. Since in addition the company will let your weeks, there is a charge of 20 per cent for this service.

The Timeshare Bourse Ltd is a wholly owned subsidiary of the Tourism Advisory Group.

Others active in the rental/resale field are Timeshare Transfer International who charge 20 per cent.

Timeshare Owners International Ltd is primarily an owners club which is hoping for affiliations with major developers. It has yet to start up its resale operations but at the time of publication it should, if it is going to survive, be well advanced in its activities.

Having established that the outlets for timeshare resales exist the question arises – what would be my selling price and the answer to this will be dictated largely by circumstances. In general terms most timesharers will have had the use of their timeshare for three to four years or more, and there will be considerable savings already associated with this.

For example, if the timesharer owns in a hotel complex then the equivalent cost of his family holidays over say four years would have been £3,500. In addition, his original purchase price would have appreciated by 10 per cent per annum. So if he paid £5,000 the value at the time of sale would be £7,265 plus the £3,500 he has already saved on his or her holidays by being an owner.

The margin therefore leaves ample room for manoeuvre and even if a 20 per cent commission is paid on the sale the net receipt of £5,812 still shows a profit on the purchase price with the holiday cost savings still intact.

Most resorts will advise you to sell at list price since any discounting will have an impact on their sales and in any event once you let it be known that you will accept less than the listed price the pressure will be on to make you discount further.

On the other hand you may be holding a prime week (see Timeshare Calendar on pp. 82-3: half-term week 8, Easter weeks 14, 15 and 16, Spring Holiday week 22 (or 21), Summer weeks 29–35, Mid-term week 43 or Christmas/New Year weeks 51–2 and 1) and if your resort is sold out you are in a good position to exact a premium over list.

Other considerations will be the status of your resort. Is it highly regarded? Is there a Phase 2 (or 3 or 4) planned? Is it nearing sell-out? Has it lived up to its promises in amenities and services?

All these questions and more will determine how soon and how well you dispose of your holding. Of course the longer you can keep it the more it will appreciate (other factors being equal) and if there is a reliable and consistent letting service it may pay you to use this whilst you wait.

Finally do not forget to tell your friends that you want to sell, since developers will tell you that more and more sales are coming from referrals and each timesharer is currently worth two and a half sales according to the statistics.

If you are at a party, on the golf course, at the tennis club or even at work, take a few minutes to tell them – and more importantly why, especially if it is a sudden reason for selling soon after purchasing. You will save on commission and friends are unlikely to seek a discount.

One factor which is making more timeshare property available for resale than normal is the selectiveness of the timesharers themselves. Those who have owned for a few years have now seen the development of other resorts with more to offer and, having determined that they want to remain timesharers, they are selling their holdings in order to buy elsewhere. If there is an urgency about it they are often prepared to drop their price and so there are some bargains to be had in these instances.

Methods of resale are:

1. Ask your resort but do not give them exclusive resale rights.
2. Advertise in the local/national press.
3. Advertise in the specialist property magazines.
4. Sell through a broker.
5. Tell your friends – often the best source of buyers.

There is of course no reason why you cannot follow all of these routes in parallel and the first one to materialize is the one you reward.

One final point: it is conceivable that some developers may 'require you' to handle all resales through them since this would give them effective overall control. Unless this is a condition of your licence which is normally freely assignable you can, if you wish, take a firm stand and ignore it.

14 Costs and Financing

A major attraction for timesharers is that the initial costs are so low in relation to those associated with outright purchase and most early purchases are made from personal available funds.

Subsequently – assuming that their experience has been a happy one – the timesharers express an interest in extending their holdings. At this point there may be some need for financial assistance and the timesharers can be encouraged by the fact that funds are readily available from a variety of sources.

Banks

The banks which at one time were naturally reticent about financing timeshare purchase have all come round to being far more relaxed in their approach and indeed the Bank of Scotland have devised a special scheme for timesharers which is available either as a direct loan or in conjunction with a major insurance company which offers the borrower a whole life policy and a 'cash back' sum after ten years which frequently exceeds the purchase price.

The APR for such facilities is a very competitive 13.9 per cent at the time of writing but this will clearly vary according to interest rates. The major stipulation is that you have to be a home owner to qualify.

In-house Schemes

Banks also play a major role in financing in-house financial assistance packages offered by developers and these may be tailored according to status from five to ten years.

The APR will of course vary from developer to developer but where the banks are the main source of funding the rates are likely to remain competitive. Often a developer can arrange a personalized service whereby the potential timesharer is invited to talk privately with the developer's bank manager at local level, the reasoning being that the timesharers can reveal details of their financial affairs direct without any potential loss of face.

Also, developers are not bankers and no matter how sympathetic their attitude the potential buyer is unlikely to declare the full extent of his or her financial commitments – whereas in the privacy of the bank manager's office all is revealed in total confidence.

It may be a few thousand over two or three years or it could be £20,000 over ten years. The developer need never know the details – he will simply receive a cheque from the timesharer in the normal way.

Some developers can and do provide their own finances and are geared to do this in a way that suggests they see this as a lucrative part of the sale. How lucrative may be gauged by the fact that typical APR's can fluctuate from 15 to 32 per cent.

Barratts on the other hand can arrange for their customers to borrow up to 90 per cent from the Clydesdale Bank, using their timeshare as collateral with repayments over ten years, and they have negotiated similar rates for their resorts in Spain.

Finance Houses

With so many of the large insurance companies taking an active part in the property market these days it is difficult to state, with any certainty who comes in this category but suffice to say perhaps that there are various schemes available from diverse sources and the only principal variants will be the rates that you are asked or prepared to pay.

All lenders will naturally satisfy themselves on your financial status and your ability to repay the amounts borrowed but such is the competition between them that you can expect to receive some very attractive offers.

Do remember, however, that when you are making your calculations on repayments, ownership of several weeks will entail some hefty maintenance charges as the basic charge becomes multiplied by the number of weeks owned. Many timesharers eventually own in excess of four weeks – one actually owns twenty.

Other Costs

Having established that there are ample funds available to support your purchase of timeshare, what other costs are you likely to incur in the actual purchase?

Well, firstly there are the costs associated with the actual inspection visit which will be quite minimal in the UK since this can range from a few gallons of petrol to a rail fare and overnight accommodation.

If it entails a trip abroad there will be the higher costs of transportation and possibly several nights' accommodation. In any event, if you purchase you will probably find that the developer will either refund or make a contributions towards your viewing expenses: much will depend on the value of your purchase. Do not expect too much in this area however since developers will not have the margins that are available when you buy a property outright.

Some developers will subsidize overnight stays but generally any significant contribution to viewing expenses will rest on whether you buy or not. Developers are all too aware of the 'professional viewers' who move from one resort to another taking whatever perks they can get along the way without any intention of buying anything.

If they have children they always want to view at Easter,

Whitsun or during the mid-term breaks. If there are no children then they are invariably retired and have a planned itinerary taking them from one resort to another with the minimum of travelling time in between.

Most developers have devised a series of questions at the booking stage which immediately flush out these time-wasters, and this, together with a quick telephone call to other developers, helps to keep it under control.

When, for example, the question 'What time of the year were you thinking of buying?' produces an answer of 'We are really quite flexible and any time could suit us', the developer is immediately on his guard since experience has shown that genuine prospective timesharers have given the matter a lot of thought before they view and all of these would have responded with answers like: 'We thought Week 43 or even Week 8 if you have any', or 'Not mid-Summer. We are anxious to avoid the crowds but June or September would be fine.'

A few simple questions of this nature can be most revealing and the developer then knows how to proceed. Very occasionally a genuine buyer will confound the screening but the developer probably feels it is worth the risk to avoid the time and expense of negative presentations.

Developers are frequently asked, 'How much will it cost me in total?' Can you give me a breakdown as, say, compared with buying a place outright?'

This puts the developer on the spot since he does not want to appear evasive but knows that the prospect expects an answer – even though there is no direct comparison since whole ownership gives the right of whole occupancy while timeshare only gives that right of occupancy associated with the weeks purchased.

Having made that point the comparison would resemble that shown in Table 1.

Many timesharers today are recruited from the ranks of disillusioned second-home owners who are only too aware of the hidden extras associated with outright purchase both in the UK and abroad but who still like it spelt out for them even though they know that there is no really true comparison.

Table 1: Extra costs

	Timeshare £15,000 (2 weeks) £		Outright purchase £40,000 £	
Viewing	150	(Part refundable)	375	(Part refundable)
Legal fees (taxes etc.)	–	(Absorbed by developer)	3,200	(8% incl.)
Insurance	–	(Absorbed by developer)	200	(House contents)
Connection (water/electricity)			60	
Furnishing	–		4,000	
Management fee	240		–	
	390	(Possibly £100 refunded)	7,835	Possibly £250 refunded)

Perhaps this is so because they are seeking confirmation that there are no hidden costs related to timeshare. Since we are concerned with costs, either at the time of purchase or in the first year, the exchange club subscription has been omitted as this – in the first year – will be borne by the developer; thereafter it is around the £50 mark and increasing.

The figure given for outright purchase assumes a very modest villa in Spain inclusive of the plot. Anything more ambitious would probably involve the separate purchase of the plot at around £15,000 plus 12 per cent land value added tax (LVA) and the cost of the villa which – according to type, number of bedrooms and quality of finish – would range from £30,000 to around £80,000 in the popular band. This too is subject to LVA but at the lower rate of 6 per cent.

Tax Implications

When purchasing a property outright in the UK the purchaser knows that there is a tax liability in terms of inheritance tax (which now replaces capital transfer tax) and, although the threshold levels are subject to adjustment by the Chancellor of the Exchequer each year, they still do not match the rate at which property prices are increasing; we are all being urged by our financial advisers to take steps now rather than leave our descendants a hefty tax bill.

Inheritance tax is normally only charged on death on gifts made within seven years of death and on lifetime gifts into certain trusts.

Even for people with only modest estates the tax can be a real burden as Tables 2 and 3 show.

Table 2: Inheritance tax rates on death

Gross transfers (£000)	Rate (%)	Cumulative tax
0–90	Nil	Nil
90–140	30	15,000
140–220	40	47,000
220–230	50	102,000
330 plus	60	

Table 3: Transfers made within 7 years of death

Years	Relief
0–3	Nil
3–4	20
4–5	40
5–6	60
6–7	80

Source: for Tables 2 and 3: Stoy Hayward.

Should a husband and wife each give £3,000 to an adult child each year for ten years they will have disposed of £60,000 worth of assets – a saving of £36,000 on inheritance tax which might otherwise have been payable on death.

Perhaps not so commonly known is the fact that gifts

Understanding the Structure of Timeshare

given in consideration of a marriage are exempt from inheritance tax up to £5,000 so that if each parent of the happy couple were to give them £5,000 each they could walk up the aisle with £20,000 tax free in their pockets and no doubt big smiles on their faces. But a word of caution here: it must be before the marriage, not after.

Capital gains tax, on the other hand, is levied on any increase in the value of an item between when it was acquired and when it was disposed of. Fortunately there are a great number of exemptions, of which private property in the form of the family home is one. It must be proven, however, that the property is the family's main home or only home throughout the time they have owned it.

The rate is 30 per cent and there is an annual exemption per individual or married couple of £6,000 whilst trustees are allowed £3,300. Furthermore there is retirement relief at the age of 60 (or earlier on grounds of ill health) of £125,000.

Where overseas property is concerned there are the twin problems of tax payable in the UK (since it is where you are domiciled that counts) and local taxes that may be due under certain circumstances.

Of paramount importance however is the security of title, and anyone buying property in Spain or Portugal – including timeshare – is strongly urged to make out a will at the time of purchase giving title to a named person, be it a surviving spouse or child of the marriage.

There is, it should be said, a complex set of rules governing these respective tax laws which go well beyond the scope of this book, requiring qualified interpretation in individual cases. To generalize about them here would only confuse and probably mislead.

So how is timeshare property regarded in the tax treatment? Well, in the case of a 'right to use' licence it is not residential property in the normal way and is simply a shared facility for which you have been granted a licence. Indeed in many ways it is akin to making a hotel booking many years ahead and paying for it in advance to guard against inflation.

It has an asset value of course and in the event of your

demise it will become part of your estate and ownership will pass to your heirs. If you want to be more specific and if there is more than one heir, then you can split the timeshare holding between them by making reference to this in your will.

At this point of course the inheritance tax will apply and how deeply it bites will depend on what steps you have taken to soften the blow.

To date the UK inspectors have not seen fit to tax timeshare holdings under any specific category as long as it is taken up under a licence and not held in title as a property. Even then title is not solely held and it becomes, for tax purposes, a divided property so that there is no clear category under which this can be taxed.

So for the moment then timeshares have been purchased and sold without attracting the attention of Her Majesty's tax officers and we can only hope that this will continue to be the case for some time to come. There is already a VAT element included in the sales price and the management fee but there the position rests.

Revenue obtained from letting timeshare is another area to consider and is obviously taxable, the onus for declaration being on the timesharer. There is no obligation on the developers for their making any returns to the Inland Revenue in this connection and it therefore becomes a matter of conscience on the part of the timesharer alone.

Many timesharers of course avoid this complication by making private arrangements with friends to exchange properties without commercial considerations of any kind so that liability is avoided.

15 Comparisons with Other Holidays

Firstly, there is the obvious cushion against inflation which a timeshare purchase provides and the following examples highlight this.

	Holiday hotel* (mid-season accommodation for 4 people)	Typical timeshare (mid-season once-and-for-all price per week)	Typical timeshare (estimated maintenance fee per week)
1984	706.86	4,290.00	91.00
1985	777.55	–	96.00
1986	855.30	–	102.85
1987	940.83	–	113.14
1988	1,034.91	–	124.45
	———Break even———		
1989	1,138.41	–	136.89
1990	1,252.25	–	150.58
1991	1,377.47	–	165.64
1992	1,515.22	–	182.21
1993	1,666.74	–	200.43
Total	11,264.54	4,290.00	1,363.19

* Source: Hotel Tariff Study of Great Britain, 1983.

The hotel category chosen in the example is 3-star, so costs would be very much higher if you went more 'up market'.

Example 1

Timeshare – Easter week purchase at say £5,000
Assume 40 years as period of tenure
Therefore £5,000 div. by 40 = £125 + management fee = £235 p.w.
Suite sleeps 6, so £235 div. by 6 = *£39 per person per week*

Loss of interest on capital invested is offset by:
   (a) profit if held for, e.g., 10 years (prices likely to double)
   (b) holiday savings (at least £1,000 p.w. in a 5-star hotel)

So

Original purchase price	£5,000
Resale price (10 years)	£10,000
Profit	£5,000
Plus 10 years' holiday use	£10,000
	£15,000
Less 10 × £250 p.a. interest loss	£2,500
	£12,500

Example 2

Assume sold your Easter week after 10 years, during which you let it 3 times. Calculation is therefore:

Profit

From sale of week	£5,000
Savings on holidays	£7,000
Revenue (net) from lets	£2,400
	£14,000
Less loss of interest	£2,500
	£11,900

Example 3

Assume you sold after 10 years, during which:

Let 3 times at £800 net
Exchange 3 times overseas resort
Profit is therefore:

From sale of week	£5,000
Savings on holidays (UK)	£4,000
Savings on holidays (overseas)	£4,500
	(2 for 1 exch)
	£13,500
Less loss of interest	£2,500
	£11,000

These examples demonstrate all too clearly the obvious financial benefits involved and the permutations are endless – but beyond this there is another major benefit to be enjoyed. If you purchase a second holiday home unless you sell you are tied to this irrevocably for life, facing all the costs of upkeep, a large capital sum tied up that could have been earning interest, and all the worries of break-ins and the increasing fears of vandalism.

It is likely, is it not, that your visits will be restricted to two or three times a year, and if you let it the wear and tear factor can be very high, or the managing company will take all the profit.

With timeshare you have the freedom of going somewhere new every year through the exchange facility if you choose, have no management worries and no cares about break-ins and the like. You also have the bulk of the money you would have laid out still available for investment or leisure.

Your membership of the exchange club will also bring you fringe benefits such as cheaper air fares, discounts on hire cars, and other attractive packages which are certain to emerge.

So much for comparison with a hotel holiday in the UK but what about other forms of holidays?

Package Tours (by Air)

Some of us prefer the convenience of walking into our local travel agents, collecting a handful of brochures and then spending the winter evenings trying to decide just where and when we would like to go. After several evenings and a bit of research we have it all clear in our minds and back we go to the travel agent to make our booking.

At this point all our careful planning, arguing and even wheedling seems to be to no avail as the holiday of our choice is either not available at the time we wanted it, at the hotel we had chosen, or with our favourite tour operator, or even in the resort of our choice.

Back we go then with another set of brochures to a cool reception from the family and more evenings of research.

Eventually we find an agreed second choice and more confidently we return to the agent who shakes his head sadly, punches away at a computer VDU (without ever telling you what he or she is doing – or the result) and generally gives you a lot of seemingly unrelated information about other areas and resorts.

Finally you leave it to them and accepting the admonishment that you are far, far too late for this or that

4-star hotel (2 weeks)	Half board £	Full board £
2 adults	934	1,260
3 children	879	1,377
	1,813	2,637
Insurance (5 ×£18)	90	90
Airport taxes (5 × £9)	45	45
Car hire (1 week)	260	260
Single room supplement	160	160
	2,369	3,192

resort you return yet again to a decidedly frosty reception to relate the bad news: 'We can't go to the Canaries – it has to be Cyprus – and in August.'

Then, having survived the outburst of 'Much too hot', 'Far too crowded', 'They don't do paella' and 'Far too expensive', you settle down to work out the cost.

In the end you opt for half board and restrict the car hire to the second week, hoping that buses or taxis will get you to where you want to go during the first. Even so there will not be much change from £3,000 and with the temperatures well up into the nineties not much opportunity for prolonged sun-bathing either.

Of course, there are cheaper package holidays available according to the time of the year that you are able to travel but where there is a family situation with children of school age this tends to restrict it to the school holiday periods which are generally the most expensive. Research any of the package tour brochures and using the family situation given in this example you are likely to come up with similar calculations.

Independent Holidays

Although a cost-comparison cannot possibly be made conclusively since it depends so much upon the type of holiday taken, we will look at a fairly typical example.

For some, part of the holiday atmosphere is captured in the pre-planning. There are destinations to be chosen, routes to be worked out, ferries to be booked, currency and passports to be organized. Then of course the car must be thoroughly checked, new maps and phrase books to be bought, and general provisions stockpiled.

Assume that the same family are using the family car, a Volvo estate to take them on a three-week journey to a self-catering holiday in Javea on the Costa Blanca. Two weeks are to be spent in the resort where they have rented a villa sleeping up to six and the other week in travelling. Again they are restricted to a late July departure and this is reflected in the costs.

The villa which has a small private pool comes with all

linen and maid services for £265 per week and the costings for the entire trip are:

Petrol	(Average price £1.85 per gallon) 2,600 miles (24 mpg)	£200
Ferry	There are at least five choices of route including the most expensive (Plymouth to Santander in Northern Spain, which then reduces the driving to 500 miles). Peak fares will apply and £280 each way will be typical to transport the car and family on the less expensive crossings.	£560
Hotel	Two overnight stops each way are needed and even at the most modest levels of accommodation £80 per night would be the likely cost.	£320
Meals en route	Experienced travellers usually manage to go a long way on their own supplies but even so a low budget would allow for £10 per head per day.	£200
Villa	(With pool and maid service) £265 per week.	£530
Food and Entertainment	Even allowing for the fact that travelling by car enables the transportation of tinned foods and provisions, local purchases of fresh food can still mount up, especially when one is in a holiday mood.	£350
		£2,160

These then represent the main types of holiday which will be compared to timeshare and although it can always be argued that you can do it cheaper, the question remains that if you are setting out to make this family holiday even better than the last, do you want to?

One fact remains indisputable: when the holiday is over, all that will be left are the memories – the money has gone forever. With timeshare you can repeat the process year in year out for virtually your original outlay and you still have an appreciating asset so that when the time comes for you to sell you will have had as savings all the money you would have spent on holidays, plus an asset which has probably appreciated by ten per cent each year.

16 Management Arrangements

In purchasing your timeshare you will have invested a modest sum either for the freehold or the licensed right to use, and the theory is that this should be your only capital outlay (capital outlay being defined as, e.g. £1,000+) during the lifetime of the project and beware of any project that does not gear its management fees to the retail price index (RPI) or whatever similar yardstick is used in the country of purchase.

The management fee is what you pay annually to the management company appointed by the developer to look after the upkeep and day-to-day running of the project. Each year it is uplifted by the percentage of the RPI and it is necessary to take a close look at what you are actually paying for.

It is totally wrong for example to judge one management fee against another until you know for certain what it encompasses. Management fees are wide-ranging both in the UK and abroad and a useful check-list will be found on page 116 to enable you to make valid comparisons.

Since more and more professional people are buying timeshare today there is a greater awareness of what is needed to ensure the viability of a project over a number of years and instances have occurred in which potential timesharers have turned down a purchase because, in their judgment, the management fees being asked were insufficient to sustain it at the standards expected throughout its lifetime.

Does the management fee, for example, allow for the replacement of the furniture and fittings on a regular basis

– say every ten years – and has a reserve fund been created for this purpose? It is common practice in the better-run developments for a percentage of the annual fee paid by the timesharer to be set aside in this way and this is a question well worth your asking.

Are the property and its contents well covered for insurance? To be more specific, your timeshare is normally part of the main building and you need to know that the superstructure is well insured so that in the event of a fire or any other calamity the structure or fabric of the building is well covered.

If the roof is torn off in a mini-tornado, for example, you do not want to be faced with a bill for several hundred pounds (or millions of pesetas or escudos) for your contribution towards putting it right.

Are the contents adequately insured and under what circumstances would you be expected to pay for any damage? A general rule here is that if you are going to break something, make a proper job of it and break something big like a television or a glass door or table! These items are well insured whereas, since it is prohibitive in premium terms for a developer to cover every tiny item, a cup or wine glass broken will be charged to you personally.

Is there third party liability cover and what is the extent of the cover? If you drop something from the window of your apartment onto somebody's head, he or she, apart from seeing it as an unfriendly gesture, is likely to sue. A frivolous example perhaps but you can never have too much insurance.

One hotel even covers you for loss of use so that, in the event of your suite not being available for reasons beyond your control, you are given the rental value of the suite (usually £1,000+) and a lot of assistance to find alternative accommodation.

Actually you are likely to be offered first an alternative suite, then, if one is not available, accommodation in the hotel with food thrown in as compensation, and finally if all else fails the value of your suite in published rental terms, with help to find suitable accommodation to save your holiday from being ruined. It must be said however that to date this has never happened – but the facility is there.

What maid services are available and what is the basis of their services? Are they daily or weekly and what supplements are charged should you want more?

Are community charges taken into account? The cost of landscape gardening, daily cleaning of the pool and refuse collection can be very heavy if charged as an extra.

Are television rentals included? What about telephones and local rates and taxes? These are all pertinent and you must establish if they are included. Then there are things like electricity, water and gas supplies – any one of these can make a big hole in your pocket if billed separately.

All of the foregoing have to be paid for and you need to know that adequate provision has been made to meet these costs; otherwise the project is certain to flounder after a few years when the initial euphoria has evaporated and then it is the task of the timesharers to bail it out.

Almost as important as what is included is what *is not included*. For instance if there is a major breakdown such as a lift needing replacement or a boiler goes on the blink, who pays for the replacements? What spares are carried in stock and if not then how soon can these be supplied – and at whose cost?

What about pets – are these allowed or is it made clear that they are not (in the agreement, for instance)? So many timesharers have been greatly distressed to find that on arrival at their resort their pet dogs or cats are barred.

Most resorts do not accept pets and understandably so when one considers the luxurious standards of decor, but some salesmen, eager to make sales, conceal the fact and heartbreak is the end result.

Some resorts however make it clear that pets are not allowed in the accommodation but have taken the time and trouble to seek out local kennels where they may be boarded so that timesharers can spend their days with their pets if they wish and board them out overnight.

Instinct, and your specific areas of interest, will guide you in the direction of the questions you ask and your confidence will either grow or recede according to the answers you receive.

Understanding the Structure of Timeshare

It is a sad fact that buyers of timeshare readily part with the cash for the purchase with only a superficial investigation of the management company, and the fees they charge, yet it is this that in the long term will decide the success of the project.

General standing and reputation

Track record
What is the reputation of the company or organization from whom you are buying? How long have they been established and how have they handled their affairs in this time? Are they the type of people with whom you would want to be associated on a long-term basis? Do you consider them trustworthy and can you verify what you are being told? If you have serious doubts then a search of the company accounts will either confirm them or set your mind at rest. Most reputable companies will allow you to inspect their last set of accounts whilst you are there but do not expect to take them away.

Quality of management
Within the period of your agreement the management will change – possibly several times, so that your reaction to the present management can only be a guide.

Look for a well-planned, well-thought-out basic management philosophy – one which will continue irrespective of who implements it. Be sure that the integrity is there from the outset and the ground rules, once established, will stand the test of time.

Agreements
All agreements will differ according to the developer's own situation. Some will offer shareholdings, club memberships, and even profit participation. An agreement should be like a good corset – it should be tight enough to provide security yet still give freedom of movement.

The basic rules before you sign any agreement should be 'Do I have absolute trust in the people with whom I am entering into agreement?' If the answer is 'yes' then it is the spirit of the agreement rather than the wording that counts.

Play safe though – show it to your solicitor, and have him check that the rights it grants are freely assignable in the event of your wishing to let, sell, bequeath or even give it away.

'Yours for life' is an expression you will often encounter – especially in overseas developments. There are very few benefits – good health excepted – that remain a benefit forever. Some have a nasty habit of becoming an encumbrance, particularly in a badly run, neglected development.

Make sure that the management fees are measurable against some yardstick in the country where you purchase. The cost of living might be falling in the UK but elsewhere it may be a vastly different story.

For the following examples of a management agreement and trust deed I am once again grateful to the Kilconquhar Castle Club, who allowed me to reproduce them unedited.

MANAGEMENT AGREEMENT

IT IS CONTRACTED and AGREED between KILCONQUHAR CASTLE ESTATE LIMITED incorporated under the Companies Acts and having its Registered Office at Kilconquhar Castle, Elie, Leven, Fife, as Founder Member in terms of Articles 12 and 15 of the Constitution of Kilconquhar Castle Club, whose Headquarters are at Kilconquhar Castle, aforesaid, of the one part, and Kilconquhar Castle Services Limited, incorporated under the Companies Acts and having its Registered Office at Kilconquhar Castle, Elie, Leven, Fife, (hereinafter referred to as 'the Management Company') of the other part, as follows:–

1. The Management Company will undertake on behalf of the Club and the Club hereby delegates to the Management Company the

management and administration of the whole of the Club's property at Kilconquhar Castle. Without prejudice to the said generality the Management Company will be responsible for all the items detailed in paragraphs (a) to (g) of Article 16 of the Constitution of the Club. The Management Company will use its best endeavours to ensure that the management and administration are carried out in the best interests of the members of the Club, and will effect all maintenance, repairs, redecoration and renewals as and when the same shall be necessary.
2. The Management Company shall, during the subsistence of this Agreement be entitled to exercise all the powers of the Committee in connection with the management and administration of the Club's property and affairs, including power to collect from each member, the sum or sums due by him in terms of Article 17 (f) of the Constitution of the Club which shall include the Management Company's own factorial fees for its services hereunder. As an alternative to apportioning the annual management costs amongst the members of the Club, the Management Company may arrange that each member pays a set annual management charge each year which annual management charge may be subject to review from time to time. Once such an arrangement has been entered into with the holder of a Holiday Certificate it shall be binding not only on him but also on his successors as holder or holders of the Holiday Certificate to which it relates. Such a set annual management charge would not cover any sums falling due under Article 17 (b) or (d).
3. This Agreement shall subsist for a period of Ten years from the Six day of July, Nineteen hundred and seventy eight.

4. The Management Company shall be entitled to assign their rights and obligations hereunder at any time to any other person or body provided such other person or body shall be of a responsible stature, but only with the consent of the said Kilconquhar Castle Estate Limited, which consent will not be unreasonably withheld.
5. Any dispute or difference arising out of these presents shall be referred to the decision of a single expert to be agreed between the parties or in default of agreement to be appointed on the application of either party by the President for the time being of the Law Society of Scotland to act as an expert and not an arbiter.

TRUST DEED

WHEREAS, KILCONQUHAR CASTLE ESTATE LIMITED incorporated under the Companies Acts and having its Registered Office at Kilconquhar Castle, Kilconquhar, Fife is Founder Member of a Club known as Kilconquhar Castle Club (hereinafter called "the Club") the object of which is to secure for its members joint rights of ownership of specific houses and also exclusive rights of occupation of these specific houses on a site at Kilconquhar Castle, Kilconquhar, Fife for specified periods in each year: AND WHEREAS it is provided in the Club's Constitution (a copy of which is annexed and executed as relative hereto) that the title to the heritable property of the Club shall be vested in an independent Trust Corporation for behoof of the members of the Club from time to time THEREFORE it is agreed as follows between the said Kilconquhar Castle Estate Limited acting on behalf of the Club as Founder Member in terms of Article 12 of the said Constitution (hereinafter called "the Founder") on the one part and THE ROYAL BANK OF SCOTLAND LIMITED (hereinafter called "the Bank") on the other part, in manner following:

1. The Founder hereby appoints the Bank and the Bank hereby agrees to act as Trustee on behalf of the Club and the members thereof from time to time subject to the provisions hereof. The Founder shall convey or cause to be conveyed to the Bank or its nominee the heritable property referred to in the said Constitution and which is hereinafter called "the Property".

2. The Bank shall be entitled to exercise such of the powers competent to trustees in Scotland, gratuitous or otherwise, as it may be requested in writing to exercise by the Club or its Committee or otherwise in terms of the Constitution of the Club. The Bank or its nominee shall not be bound to concur in or perform any act or acts which in the opinion of the Bank shall be illegal or shall constitute a breach of trust or shall involve the Bank or its nominee in any personal liability.

3. The Bank shall have no responsibility for the administration or management of the Property, shall not be liable for any losses or depreciation which may result in any way to the Property and gives no guarantee in regard to the validity or otherwise of the title to the Property.

4. The Bank shall not be required to take any legal action in relation to any matter whatsoever unless fully indemnified by the Club or the Founder to the reasonable satisfaction of the Bank for all costs and liabilities likely to be incurred or suffered by the Bank.

5. The Bank shall be entitled to obtain legal advice from its solicitors for the time being and/or the Opinion of Counsel on any matter relating to the Property or in relation to the Trust hereby constituted or the exercise of the Bank's powers or duties thereunder and that at the expense of the Club or the Founder.

6. The Founder hereby warrants that save as otherwise ordered by a Court of competent jurisdiction or as provided herein the Bank shall not by entering into and acting in pursuance of the terms or conditions of this Agreement owe any duty, obligation or liability to any person or persons (whether corporate or individual) other than the Club and that no such person or persons shall be entitled to charge, pledge or demand to require or oblige the Bank or its nominee to transfer any property held by the Bank or its nominee in pursuance of this Agreement.

7. The Founder hereby warrants for itself and on behalf of the Club that the Bank's name shall not appear on any literature or document or on any advertisement issued by or on behalf of the Founder or the Club without the approval in writing of the Bank having first been obtained.

8. The Bank shall not be responsible for any loss suffered by the Club or any member thereof or by the Founder arising out of or in respect of any act or omission on the part of the Bank, its officers, employees or agents in respect of the property unless the same shall have been caused by or have arisen from bad faith or negligence on the part of the Bank or its said officers, employees or agents.

9. The Founder shall pay or procure that the Club shall pay to the Bank as remuneration

Understanding the Structure of Timeshare 113

for the performance of its duties hereunder such fees as may from time to time be separately agreed upon between the Founder and the Bank which failing between the Club and the Bank and all out of pocket expenses incurred by the Bank in the performance of its duties under this Agreement. The Founder shall pay the said remuneration exclusive of Value Added Tax which shall be added at the rate applicable in the circumstances.

10. The Founder for itself and on behalf of the Club hereby indemnifies and holds harmless the Bank and its nominees from and against all costs, liabilities and expenses which may result from the performance by the Bank of its duties hereunder and the Bank shall be kept fully indemnified by the Club and the Founder against all losses, claims, demands, expenses and others made or incurred in connection with the Property or in any other way in connection with the holding by the Bank of the office of Trustee hereunder. The Bank shall have right, if at any time it considers it desirable so to do, to require that the Founder or the Club shall deposit with the Bank such sum as the Bank shall think necessary in support of the Indemnity contained in this clause.

11. This Agreement shall commence on the last date hereof and shall continue thereafter in full force and effect until terminated either by the Founder or the Club giving not less than three months' notice in writing to the Bank or by the Bank giving to the Founder and the Club not less than three months' notice in writing. Such notices shall not be given in any event before the expiry of one year from date hereof. Upon termination of this Agreement the Founder whom failing

the Club shall pay to the Bank all remuneration then owing to the Bank together with any outstanding out of pocket expenses and all expenses incurred by the Bank in conveying the title to the Property in manner after provided. The Bank shall in the event of this Agreement being terminated convey or cause to be conveyed at the expense of the Club whom failing at the expense of the Founder to any succeeding Trustee (which has entered into an Agreement with the Club and which the Founder or the Club have shown to the reasonable satisfaction of the Bank to be acceptable as Trustee to the members of the Club) or to the office-bearers for the time being of the Club, the Property, the title to which is then vested in the Bank or its nominee.

12. The Founder undertakes to give or to procure that there shall be given to the Bank the names and addresses of all office-bearers of the Club and further undertakes to inform or procure that the Bank shall be informed of any change in the holder of any office with the full name and address of each new office-bearer. The Founder shall procure that within fourteen days of the relevant meeting there shall be delivered to the Bank duly certified by the Chairman or Secretary of the Committee of the Club an excerpt from the Minute of any meeting of the Committee or of the members of the Club minuting the resignation of an office-bearer or other member of Committee or the election or appointment of a new office-bearer or committee member and any change in the Constitution of the Club approved by the members thereof. The Founder shall also procure that there shall be delivered to the Bank a copy of each Annual Audited

Account of the Club. The Bank shall be given notice of and shall have the right to attend as observer all General Meetings of the members of the Club but shall have no right to vote at any such Meeting.

13. Notwithstanding the provisions of this Agreement the Bank or any subsidiary or associated Company of the Bank shall not be precluded from acting as banker to the Founder or the Club nor shall the Bank or any subsidiary or associated company of the Bank be precluded from making any advances to the Founder or the Club on such terms as may be agreed or from making any contract or entering into any financial or other transaction in the ordinary course of business with the Founder or the Club and shall be entitled to charge interest on overdrawn accounts and to make the usual banker's charges and shall not be liable to account either to the Founder or the Club for any profit made in connection therewith.

14. Any notice which is required to be given in terms of any provision of this Agreement shall be given or served by sending the same by prepaid first class mail, telegram, cable or telex to the Founder, to the Club or to the Bank as the case may be and any notice sent by post shall be deemed to have been given or served 48 hours after despatch and any notice sent by telegram, cable or telex shall be deemed to have been given or served at the time of despatch. This Agreement shall be governed by and construed in accordance with the Law of Scotland.

Management Charges: Check-list

Item	Resort 1	Resort 2	Resort 3	Resort 4
Annual charge				
Is VAT included?				
Is it linked to RPI?				
Is there a reserve fund (refurbishment)?				
Insurance Cover Fabric of building Contents of unit Third party liability Loss of use cover				
Rates included Local rates TV rentals Telephone rentals Video rentals				
Cleaning services Weekly/daily maid service Linen/towels changed Consumables replaced Communal cleaning				
24-hour maintenance Electricity charges Gas charges Hot water Water Telephone				
Management rating 1–10				

17   Exchange Facilities

In truth even existing timesharers find it difficult to understand the exchange system but, like everything else in life, familiarity comes with use.

With RCI (Resort Condominiums International) for example the procedures for making an exchange follow this pattern and it works like a bank account.

Terminology

The 'bank account' is called the RCI Spacebank.

The 'deposit' is the holiday time you own at your resort and which you assign to RCI.

The 'withdrawal' is the like amount of holiday time and accommodation which you request from deposits made by other RCI members.

An 'accrual' is where your right to exchange is carried forward to the year following.

Options

RCI offer two options of types of holiday exchange

1. *Exchange with a different resort*
   This is where you deposit your own timeshare with RCI and then request an exchange to another resort – either in the UK or abroad.
2. *Internal exchange*
   This is when you want to holiday at your own resort but on different dates to those you own.

It would be as well to remember that exchange is a global thing and no two resorts are alike. This some might say contributes to its appeal but it is important to come away feeling that you got the best of the deal rather than the reverse.

To this end RCI and indeed II (Interval International) insist that their affiliated resorts observe a certain criteria of standards and regular inspections are made to ensure these are met. Even so a check of the resorts' amenities in the directories provided by both RCI and II will help you to decide.

Time Zones

The dates on which you occupy your timeshare will determine which zones you will be in. For example:

> *Red Zone* – is prime time and usually consists of all of the summer months plus weeks 51, 52 and 1.
>
> *White Zone* – usually covers Easter, spring and early autumn.
>
> *Blue Zone* – usually refers to the winter months and offers the least choice in exchange terms.

To get this in perspective: if you own prime time – *red* – you effectively can exchange into all of the time available since you can exchange down into the other two zones. So if there were 1,500 resorts you would have your pick, subject of course to availability.

If you own *White* time then you can exchange into all of the White and Blue Zones.

If you own *Blue* time then of course your choice can only be within the Blue Zone.

So if your motivation in buying timeshare stems from the attraction of the exchange scheme then you would be well advised to buy *Red* or prime time. Many timesharers of course own in all three zones which give them even greater flexibility of choice.

So having bought your timeshares and decided that you want to exchange, you should first check the directory provided and in the case of RCI make four selections (not necessarily in order of preference).

You should remember that your exchange requests will be matched against what you own so if you own a unit that sleeps four then you may not request a unit that sleeps six – the like-for-like principle will prevail.

Resorts are graded according to availability and you should wherever possible choose one with a high availability rating.

Another point to remember is that the RCI Spacebank is built upon listings of one week so that if you are exchanging more than one week you will need to complete a separate Spacebank request card for each week.

1. Make sure that your annual subscription is paid up for the year in which you are exchanging.
2. Send your Spacebank card depositing your time owned 60 days in advance.

When this is received RCI will check it carefully against its records and when verified that all is in order it will be entered into its Spacebank Pool (computer). Once this is done you will receive an acknowledgement and the time deposited is no longer available for your own use.

If you own in a high-demand resort, then you may with confidence enclose your exchange request form at the same time as you make your deposit. On this you will have listed your four choices, the size of your party and your method of travel.

With this form you must also send your exchange fee which is currently £38 per week (£75 if exchanging two weeks) if overseas, and £21 if internally (£42 if two weeks).

Some timesharers omit to send anything believing that the exchange fee is included in their annual subscription. It is not and RCI say they need this to cover the cost of the computer time and administration.

What now happens is that the computer (the Spacebank Pool) is asked two main questions.

1. Is the time requested available in any of the resorts listed?
2. Does RCI have timesharers wait-listed to take up the time offered?

If the answers are yes on both counts then you will receive written confirmation of your exchange and you can now make your travel arrangements.

Do not under any circumstances make your travel arrangements until you receive this confirmation in writing.

Do not accept any verbal assurances – these are likely to be hard to pin down if there is any snag.

Should RCI be unable to arrange an exchange then your deposit (time owned) will be returned and the fees refunded.

Some resorts are affiliated to RCI but are still under construction and have a 'presale status'. If you have bought or are thinking of buying into one of these then it is unlikely that you may exchange until this has been lifted.

You may also have requested an exchange and in the interim stage sold or upgraded your unit. You must advise both RCI and the developer of the status at the time of purchase or sale.

If you are obliged to cancel a confirmed exchange then do remember that fees are non-refundable on confirmed exchanges – and equally the time deposited is also not refundable.

Several options are offered by RCI so that you do not lose out completely but there is also a special timesharer's insurance available that might be useful on these occasions – rare though they may be. You can have your week(s) back of course if it/they have not already been allocated.

There are some basic differences between the RCI and II systems and without going into detail which would only confuse the reader it is enough to say that they each work effectively in providing the benefits that their members expect.

II do not, for example, operate a space bank like RCI and

Understanding the Structure of Timeshare 121

they rely instead on their members sending in their exchange requests well before the dates on which they wish to travel. Only when they are able to confirm the exchange will they accept their member's week on deposit – their reasoning being that in this way they are safeguarding holidays that might otherwise be lost.

The overall benefit to the timesharer must be that each organization lays down strict rules on standards and to remain affiliated the developer must observe those at all times.

Both clubs are able to offer discounts on travel through their association with various companies or agents, RCI with Viking and II with Holiday Fax.

RCI are also able to offer a comprehensive insurance holiday cover which gives the timesharer, forced to cancel, the alternative of another holiday or financial reimbursement.

II operate a grading scheme for their resorts with the better ones classified as 5-star whilst RCI give awards of a 'Resort of International Distinction' to their top establishments.

Ultimately it seems inevitable that all resorts will be graded and this will rule out for ever the practice of some timesharers buying the cheapest they can with a view to exchanging into the top resorts.

This however tends to be self-regulating in that exchanges into these top resorts are already very difficult and are restricted to those members who qualify by virtue of having bought like time at like value elsewhere.

It is unlikely that either RCI or II would agree with this statement but developers are in a strong position, particularly the nearer they get to sell-out, to influence outcome.

It is not possible, even with a cash adjustment, to exchange up into another colour band and you should be very wary of any salesman's assurances that you can.

So much bad feeling has already been caused by salesmen who have sold cheap low season weeks, in some remote locality, to their customers on the basis that they need not take it up but can exchange it for prime weeks elsewhere.

There have been several instances reported recently whereby timesharers have bought in the Canaries and Portugal and presented themselves at the resort demanding an exchange into a penthouse in the peak of the season.

Investigations revealed that each had been told at the point of sale that this was their right and it could not be challenged. In each case the weeks they had purchased were in the Blue band, the price paid was around £1,000 and the terms 'like value in a similar time period' were not even understood.

Not only that but no approach had been made to the exchange club in the first instance to ascertain if an exchange was possible. Had they done so then they would have very quickly been set straight on the correct procedures.

No explanations had been given at the time and there was genuine belief that the first approach was to the resort to agree when they could come and then notify the exchange club.

We can only assume from these and other similar experiences that some timeshare resorts do not feel any responsibility for explaining the exchange systems and probably regard this as detracting from their sales effort.

Certainly the salesmen questioned seemed ill-informed and impatient, being more concerned with closing the sale than providing satisfactory answers to questions in this area. Since exchange is such an excellent sales tool this does seem short-sighted but that is a matter for the developers who determine their sales policies to sort out.

Summary

1. Buy your timeshare at an affiliated resort.
2. When you wish to exchange, select the resort(s) you want to visit from the directory provided.
3. Deposit your week(s) with the exchange club who will bank it with their computer.
4. The exchange club computer then checks that the resort is vacant at the time you want to visit and that they have timesharers waiting to take up your week(s).

5. You receive confirmation and all you then have to do is make your travel arrangements. Even here the exchange club can help you through their associated travel departments.

Since well over ninety per cent of exchange requests are confirmed, your chances are very good unless of course you want to go to a European ski resort during the height of the season. In this instance experience has shown that purchasers of timeshare in ski resorts do so because they have every intention of using it.

Without doubt then the exchange facility is vital to the future prosperity of the timeshare industry and we can anticipate considerable growth in the numbers of affiliations and the travel packages to enable timesharers to enjoy cost-effective mobility.

PART THREE
Choosing Your Timeshare

18 Location – Where Do I Buy my Timeshare?

In an age of space travel this becomes increasingly difficult to answer and I suppose the best reply, assuming all else is equal is: 'Where you feel most comfortable about your investment.'

It is a great temptation when the sun is on your back and the champagne flowing to buy on impulse in some faraway spot. A decision taken through some alcoholic haze is never one of your best and all too often these are deeply regretted.

If statistics are anything to go on most people buy within three hours' travel from where they live – which in itself opens up a very wide spectrum.

In more recent times and with the advent of the exchange clubs, buyers have shown a marked preference to buy into a development which can be reached easily so that they may make regular and often unannounced visits when not in residence to check out their investments.

Cost must play a part in this so normally it involves a drive by car of up to three hours – lunch at the resort followed by a quick chat with the management and timesharers in residence, an inspection of the project and a return drive the same day.

It becomes a very pleasant family outing which is frequently extended to a weekend break and the end result is nearly always the same – a warm endorsement of the earlier decision to purchase in that particular resort.

This trend is responsible for the growth of UK resorts from one to forty plus in eleven years since money invested at home is generally held to be a sounder investment than that invested abroad.

After all, the argument is that when you have the urge to seek pastures new you can make use of the exchange facilities so that in the words of RCI, 'Your timeshare purchase becomes your passport to the world.'

Contrast this with a purchase of timeshare abroad and the first thing you have to face if you intend an interim inspection trip is the time scale. Even if you live adjacent to one of the major airports you will be facing earlier and earlier checking in times as security measures are tightened further.

For cost reasons you will probably be travelling by a charter flight offering reduced air fares and if so then flight delays are inevitable – often up to several hours, both ways.

My wife and I, for example, recently made a same-day inspection trip to La Manga in Spain. The flight by British Midland was scheduled to take off at 9.30 so it meant rising at 5.30 and leaving home at 6.30 to arrive at Heathrow at 8.30.

There was an hour's delay before take off so we left Heathrow at 10.30 bound for the regional airport of Murcia, twenty miles or so from La Manga. En route we were informed that because of a military exercise the airport at Murcia was closed to us and that we would instead be flown to Alicante and coached from there to La Manga.

We duly arrived at Alicante at 1300 hrs GMT and set out for La Manga by coach. Eventually after a totally boring drive which seemed to be at a snail's pace, we arrived at La Manga at 1430 GMT but 1530 local time.

On arrival we were made very welcome by the management who had been waiting hours for us to appear. We were hastily bundled into a meeting room for an address by various project executives and some very patient Spanish regional officials.

At 1615 local time we were offered lunch on the terrace on a lovely day but told we must finish in twenty minutes in order to keep to the programme. We learned later that this was originally scheduled to be a two-hour affair.

Suffering from chronic indigestion we were then bundled into our coaches once more and taken at the double on a lightning tour of the project.

In all we spent one and a half hours on site before being whisked away – this time to the airport at Murcia where our aircraft was scheduled for a 1900 hrs take off. Because of a mix-up over tickets we were delayed until 2000 hrs local time by which time we had missed our slot in air traffic control.

We eventually landed at Heathrow at 2200 hrs GMT and after the usual baggage delays, customs clearance and finding our car we left for home at 2315 hrs – arriving back at 0130 hrs – shattered and having seen nothing.

The point of this story is that in order to spend one and a half hours on site we had travelled for sixteen hours and one can only feel sympathy for the management of the project who had spent so much time and money in preparing a welcome for us, only to have to abandon all of their plans in order to comply with the flight restriction.

Yes, it was ambitious to try and squeeze it into one day but what chance did they have when things started to go wrong?

I have listened to similar stories over the past five years told by timesharers who have bought abroad and have ample first-hand experience of my own to draw on. All of which only serves to confirm that the travel factor must be taken into account when contemplating overseas purchase and we have not even touched on our traffic-control strikes, fog or other adverse weather conditions – and that old chestnut 'delays due to aircraft operational difficulties' or 'delays due to the late arrival of the incoming aircraft'.

Then there is the question of cost. As soon as you announce your intention to take a quick peek at what you have bought the whole family want to come and then of course there is not much point in going for a couple of days – not all that way – so before you know it you are faced with financing an extra holiday just to check out the timeshare that was going to save you money on holidays.

And when you get there, who do you talk to? That nice Señor Garcia who speaks such good English is with clients or away visiting his sister in the north (always in the north?) but do not despair his assistant Señorita Herrero is there to help you:

'*Señorita*, the pool seems very dirty and some of the sun beds are broken. Why is this?'

'Señor Garcia – he no here. Maybe next week.'

'Yes, we know that Señor Garcia is away but where is your maintenance man?'

'He north – visit sister. Come back next week.'

'No, not Señor Garcia. Your maintenance man – where is he?'

'*No comprendo, Señor – habla Español?*'

'No, I do not speak Spanish. Is there anyone else we can talk to?'

'Señor Garcia – he come back next week.'

At this point we British – who are not the most tolerant of people – tend to get louder and louder but all to no avail and after two or three days prowling around the site getting more and more riled by what we see we give up and head for home where we write seven-page letters full of complaints to which we get no replies.

So an expensive inspection visit can prove abortive and we are left to thrash it all out during our period in residency when hopefully Señor Garcia will be on site to hear our complaints and to offer satisfaction.

Of course it is possible to buy overseas and not experience these problems. Many large companies have established overseas timeshare operations which have first-class people running them and these give every satisfaction. That makes it doubly important to be selective in your choice and ensure that you do not encounter the difficulties that can occur if you are not.

19 *What Do I Look for when Buying Timeshare?*

In contrast with outright purchase where the ground rules related to property buying have long since been clearly established, the purchase of timeshare is, for many of us, breaking new ground.

This is also particularly true of our solicitors since they are aware of their responsibility to advise correctly on a topic of which they have little or no experience. It might well be that their client will bring them a timeshare licence and ask them for an appraisal and this could be the first request of this nature they have received.

Some, it must be said, take a negative view because their overall impressions, based largely on hearsay, are unfavourable but the majority seek to learn more and advise on the soundness or otherwise of what is being presented. Indeed many go on to become timesharers themselves and some resorts boast a high number of solicitors amongst their customers.

But before the potential purchaser gives his solicitor any documents to read he should him or herself be alerted to the type of questions to ask and whatever documents he or she is ultimately asked to sign should be referred, before signature or commitment, to a member of the legal profession in the country of purchase.

Some people feel – and indeed are deliberately made to feel – that they will appear ignorant if they ask simple questions but it is your money you are spending so keep asking your questions until you get satisfactory answers.

Do not be fobbed off with inadequate replies – you want

to understand what is on offer and the vendor has a duty to ensure that you do.

What Is the Company Structure – and Who Is the Owner?

It is important to get this right at the outset. Who are you buying from? How long have they been established? Do they own the site or if it is leasehold how long is the lease? Do they have clear title to the property or does the bank have first charge? Does the period on offer fall within the lease held by the owners and will a new lease be negotiated?

It is quite common to find that many reputable businesses are operated leasehold and you should not be put off simply because a property is leasehold rather than freehold just as long as the period of the lease held exceeds by five years the period of the licence offered to you.

You will find that timeshare sold in perpetuity (for life) is possible in the USA, on the Continent and in Scotland but not in England and Wales where the laws against perpetuity forbid it. All timeshare sold in England and Wales therefore is on a right-to-use basis.

What Are You Buying?

In viewing a project the chances are that you will be shown a variety of units varying in size, layout, design, inventory and location. Not surprisingly when you sit down to finalize you can be a little confused by the talk of units, suites, apartments, terrace, patio, ground floor and Phases I, II or III etc.

Ask for a plan drawing of what you are buying (there is bound to be one) and an inventory. Make it clear at the time that you will expect to see both attached to any agreement you eventually sign so that there can be no confusion in anyone's minds.

A good tip is to initial both the plan and then the inventory – then ask for photocopies.

How Long Has It Been On the Market?

This will give you some valid feel for whether or not it has been a successful project. Too short a period – say, under three years – and it will not have built up any track record or had enough market exposure.

Six or seven years and it could be that sales are not going as well as they would have you believe. This must be approached with caution however since many projects are built in phases and often there can be a gap of two years between phases.

Perhaps a better guide would be to ask what percentage sell-out has been achieved in each phase. Nobody is going to give you exact figures of sales value but most are happy to quote a percentage.

The better project will never reveal the identity of their customers so do not be put off if you get a flat refusal in this area – after all, they will give you the same protection and if you are a celebrity it is a comfort to know that the management are not about to make capital out of that fact and leave you to face fans who have been alerted to when you will be there just when all you want is absolute privacy.

Are Any Further Phases Planned?

It is very important to know this for a variety of reasons and you should pursue questions around this until you are certain you have the facts. You will need to pursue them quite aggressively since the developer is likely to want to keep his options open.

I know of instances where the developer has sworn that he has no plans for further development and a year later a beach-side apartment with 180° uninterrupted views over the sea and coastline has found itself hemmed in on each side by tower blocks which obliterate all but the early morning sun and restrict views to straight ahead.

The developer had sold the land to another developer and claimed he had kept good faith because he personally did not build.

As explained earlier, your purchase will appreciate faster once sell-out has been achieved. If several further phases are planned then there is the obvious delay in this expectation but beyond that it might be that features incorporated in the new phase may make them more desirable and likely to make resales in your earlier phase more difficult.

This is not to say that your property will no longer appreciate but simply that the later phase will be more in demand, particularly when they are all sold.

Developers generally, having gained their expertise, will exploit to the hilt the planning permission opportunities on their own site, and then try to repeat this elsewhere. Mostly existing timesharers, having built up confidence in the developer, will be eager to support any new venture that is being developed and this is a sure indication that all is well on this particular project.

Of course it can be argued that the more timesharers there are on the one site the more there are to share the costs. A valid argument perhaps but equally it can mean that this places a great strain on the available amenities.

An extra tower block of seventy-two apartments having an average of four occupants per week can make a huge difference to things like sunbeds around the pool, use of saunas, jacuzzi, showers and the dressing rooms, whilst hairdressing appointments may involve long irritating delays and booking in the restaurant can become a nightmare.

Be sure then that the numbers proposed both now and in the future are not likely to swamp the available services and be sceptical about any promises to extend these if that should happen.

Is There a Management Company Appointed?

It is a standard practice within the timeshare industry for the developer to appoint a company to market the product and a management company to handle the post sales operation. Naturally the developer is eager to recover his investment in the shortest period and the sales effort is geared to this.

Much will depend on how the weeks are sold as to who handles the post-sales management and perhaps the best situation is where the developer accepts in full his responsibilities throughout the lifetime of the licence by forming a wholly owned subsidiary company with directors from its main board officiating.

In this way timesharers can deal direct with main board directors who they can be sure will pass on their views at board meetings and give them a positive influence on policy. If that subsidiary is also the marketing company then so much the better since it is highly unlikely that any promises will be made at the selling stage that cannot be substantiated.

If you buy your timeshare on a right-to-use-by-club-membership basis then the club will either become the management company or it will appoint an agent to act for it.

The theory is that you will then, as a club member, have a voice in how it is run but in practice, time and distance frequently mean that apart from major decisions your voice on matters affecting the club is in direct proportion to the amount of time you have purchased.

Some developers charge a maintenance (management) fee guaranteed not to increase by more than the percentage of the retail price index in the country of purchase for a period of five years – after which it becomes actual costs shared. This is done for two reasons.

Firstly the developer knows that it will probably take five years to achieve a sell-out and secondly, if actual costs were shared during a period when there were very few timesharers, the management fees would be out of all proportion and sales resistance would restrict progress.

The actual costs therefore for the first five years will have been calculated and incorporated in the selling price. At the end of this period a management company takes over and either operates on an annual fee allocated by the developer or operates on a cost-plus basis.

The great danger is that the developer may have set the management company a fee for their services which is unrealistic, which means that year by year the services to the timesharer suffer as the management company is forced to remain within its fee limitations.

Some developers, having made their profit on the selling operation, accept – you might even say encourage – the timesharers taking over the management and this has led to some unpleasant discoveries as timesharers' committees find that the developer has absorbed the true costs during sell-out and they have now inherited them with a vengeance.

There are other arrangements whereby your money is placed in trust and used to support and sustain the project during its lifetime. Here it is necessary for you to check that your money will be held in a client or trustee account or in escrow and be sure you know who has access to these funds.

There is little point, for example, in placing your money in a trust account if the person who controls the account is acting for the developer. And there is the question of what happens when the trust ends.

More and more timeshare is being sold, particularly in Spain, on a short-term, twenty or twenty-five years basis, after which it is sold and the proceeds distributed 'after costs' to the owners who normally are entitled to 1 per cent of the profits.

It is too early to say how owners will fare under this arrangement since property appears to be enjoying a high appreciation and as we know in many cases prices have gone through the roof.

Much will depend on its location; what has been built around it in the meantime; wear and tear on the fabric of the building(s); and its mechanical services, site maintenance, accessibility and popularity. These areas are speculative and as stated earlier, 'The only certainty in life is change.'

One factor that could alter values dramatically is political stability; another is the prevailing currency exchange rate and the economy.

The importance then of the management arrangement after sales cannot be stressed too highly and you must be satisfied that when you return each year you will be prompted to say to the management, 'it is just as it was when we bought it.'

Long-established hotels offering timeshare start out with a great advantage in this area since they know after many years of experience what materials will survive accelerated wear and tear and still look good many years on.

Their housekeepers and maids know as a matter of form what chemicals may be safely used to remove biro marks from dralon, wine stains from heavy-pile carpets and food stains from leather. The higher the standards of the hotel then the more likely that its timeshare units will reflect this – after all, looking after people and furnishing is its main activity.

Inspection Visits before Purchase

Make it a golden rule that you see what you are buying before you buy it. A beautifully presented brochure or an impressive video presentation seen in the comfort of your lounge or the off-site agent's office is no substitute for actually seeing the product.

Many are those who have bought sight unseen and lived to rue the day. The brochure or the video will not show you that your property is separated from the beach by a major arterial road that is packed with evil-smelling lorries and coaches twenty-four hours a day.

Neither will they show you that your property adjoins a ravine which carries the sewage of all the properties built on the hill behind you.

Little mention will be made of the fact that your only access to the beach is via a dank-smelling unlit tunnel under the road or that the 'quaint little fish restaurant and bar right on the beach itself' is in reality a hang-out for drop-outs and drunkards, and a target for frequent visits by the police.

The lapping of the waters on a moonlit shore can conjure up romantic visions but these disappear rapidly when local investigations show that it is totally unsafe to walk there after dark.

And how about the claim that it is only 'twenty minutes by modern highway from the airport'?

Having arrived, fought for your long-delayed luggage in the sticky heat and spent at least thirty minutes in filling in your car rental form because it is printed only in the local language, then locating your car, only to find that it is not the model ordered – too small for your party and with the seat anchorage broken away.

Eventually when you do make the highway you find that it is packed with vehicles of all descriptions and the drive to your resort is like a stock-car race with everyone trying to knock the leader off the track.

You finally arrive, shattered, and need several brandies to recover from the experience.

Indeed I know of one friend who hired a car at the airport in the manner described – drove it to the resort and never drove it again for two weeks – at the end of which time he paid the resort's gardener to take it back to the airport while he and his family went by taxi.

No, buying from a site plan is a very unrewarding experience and visiting the site itself will reveal far more than you are ever likely to discover otherwise. You might, of course, also find features which are additionally attractive and a personal inspection might make you decide to lift your sights and buy the penthouse or a three-bedroomed villa instead of the two-bedroomed one in which you were first interested.

Seeing the views from each unit inspected, examining the decor and colours used first-hand, can help you to choose the one best suited to your requirements.

If you have travelled some distance then you will in all probability be there for a few days and this will provide a further opportunity to observe the resort services in operation.

You will, if you hang around the site office long enough, learn how complaints are handled and special requirements dealt with: check on cleaning standards (particularly in the pool area) and you will also have a chance to talk with existing timesharers (make sure they are not planted by the management) and generally absorb the atmosphere.

Pay particular attention to the attitude of the staff – at all levels. If they are courteous and helpful it is usually a clue to a well-run, well-motivated establishment.

Choosing Your Timeshare 139

Check also what financial inducements there are to make an inspection visit. Most resorts will refund your flight costs when you buy whereas others in this country have very special overnight rates and make a flat contribution to your viewing expenses when you buy.

Take your time – see everything on offer and only buy when you are fully satisfied with all the answers given and even then only after you have shown the documents to your solicitor.

Summary

Travelling time
How long will it take you to get there – a matter of hours or will you be travelling all day?

Travel costs
Is it a case of a tankful of petrol to transport the whole family or several hundreds of pounds for air fares and rising each year?

Remote or central
Will you need a car when you get there, or can you leave the car parked and take a leisurely stroll to the beaches, shops, theatres and other amenities? For that matter – do you have guaranteed parking?

Good views – site value
Does your resort command a prominent and desirable position? What views are there? How valuable is the site?

Checkability
Can you visit at random during the year – to gather atmosphere and generally keep an eye on your investment?

Resale value
What are you chances of selling on in a few years – what sort of price do you think you would get?

Amenities

1. *Resort* What local amenities does the resort itself offer? Are there enough to sustain interest over a number of years?
2. *Area* Supplementing this, what amenities in general does the area offer? Will they attract you back for many years to come?
3. *Will it impress?* When your friends come to see you, are they likely to react favourably to what you bought – or will they wonder why?

Management

1. How long has the current management been in charge? If a recent appointment what happened to his or her predecessor?
2. What influence do they have with senior management? Is it a board appointment?
3. Is the management company a subsidiary or just under contract?
4. How do you rate the management team is there a good back-up by professionals?
5. What is the management's attitude? Do they appear to enjoy their work or is it a chore?
6. Is there any evidence of disharmony either amongst themselves or with their employers?
7. Is the management able to receive complaints and do they show a willingness to act upon them?

In conclusion, it might be helpful to mention a few points of special interest to those who might be contemplating the purchase of timeshare in France where it is not uncommon to discover that your timeshare is only one of the many apartments on offer in a block of flats and that the remainder are wholly owned.

This does create problems in regard to the rights you enjoy in relationship to your neighbours and any purchase of this type will require the closest scrutiny by expert eyes. The word 'propriété' appears frequently enough and this implies outright ownership whereas it should have a prefix such as *'multijouissance'* or *'multivacances'* to indicate that it is really *'time-propriété'*.

The legal profession in France has long been concerned about the vague legal arrangements which are used to grant the right to use for timeshare and more particularly so when the block of flats is occupied partly by timesharers and the remainder by those who own outright.

A new law was introduced in 1986 to overcome some of the problems but so far this has not been of much help – either to existing timesharers who are not affected or to impending timesharers who have no obligation to observe the new arrangements.

If we assume then that you are buying your timeshare from someone who himself or herself has done no more than purchase several apartments in some vast apartment block which is then sold to you on a timesharing basis, their status is that of co-propriétaire.

You would then, together with possibly fifty others, be granted the right to use in a block where the owner is no more than the co-owner, together with all the remaining co-owners. In such instances you will effectively own nothing and have little or no protection under French law.

No doubt the timesharers would be represented at co-owners' meetings but the strength of the vote they may have would be decided by the extent of their holdings.

If you are seriously thinking of making such a move then the best advice I can give is that you seek membership of the Mediterranean Property Owners' Association Ltd. which is an English company with fully qualified representation in France.

For a small annual fee they can guide your steps in respect of the many problems both potential and real that arise from co-ownership in France. The same organization is also represented in Spain.

20 Consumer Protection

Clearly as the industry continues to develop and expand there is the need for a 'watchdog committee' to safeguard the interests of the timesharers themselves and those of the developers who after all have invested many millions to provide the facilities.

The first of these to surface in the UK was the British Property Timeshare Association but its initial code of practice was not all-embracing enough to meet the needs of the majority of developers and it lacked support from the big names in the industry.

In recent times it made attempts to re-establish itself but faced competition from the European Holiday Timeshare Association, which encompassed the European scene, and also from the Timeshare Developers Group. The latter was a small group of the larger names in the industry who were anxious to stem the adverse criticism being levelled at the tactics of one or two developers.

It is interesting to see how each of these associations, and perhaps others that follow, set about dealing with the problems of irresponsible developers and become accepted both as the authority and the voice of the industry.

At present it would appear that terms of membership are structured around the interests of the largest members rather than the wider need for strong policing in the interests of all.

The danger is that potential timesharers may be influenced by affiliations to one or other of these associations without realizing that such affiliations are largely meaningless and will remain so until the code of practice receives full support from the industry and effective means of policing are introduced.

For example, any trade association formed states its objectives and its code of practice. It sets out its stall as the voice of the industry and represents its members' interests in all matters related to their operations, and advises on trends and legislation. Membership must be a status symbol and ultimately mandatory to acceptance of the user.

Currently individual developers are all doing their own thing without any co-ordination, and no effective means have been found to curb and eliminate the high-pressure tactics employed – even by the larger companies operating in Spain, Portugal and the Canaries, and now appearing in the UK.

The trade association must be able to obtain members' agreement to abide by its principles and objectives, and also be capable of imposing fines upon those members who stray. Failure to pay a fine would normally result in a member being 'blacklisted' and expelled from the association.

Such a move would have serious repercussions on a member's ability to trade since potential timesharers would be encouraged to check out a member's status before making a purchase.

Regrettably we have a long way to go before reaching such a situation and many of the more creditable developers are still operating independently, and predictably will continue to do so until they can see some real benefits in applying for membership.

There can be little doubt that if the industry is to survive and prosper a strong trade association is vital and one which will receive the necessary support and serve the best interests of both the developer and the timesharer.

An amalgamation of the three associations – The British Property Timeshare Association, The European Holiday Timeshare Association and The Timeshare Developers Group – now exists under the banner of The Timeshare Developers Association. Each country will be responsible for the activities of its own developers and their efforts will be co-ordinated by an international timeshare body. Meanwhile the governments of the offending countries should 'boot out' those companies who are bringing the industry into disrepute.

So what steps should a potential timesharer follow to ensure protection? Well, you cannot go far wrong by applying to the English Tourist Board for its leaflet, 'Code of Caution and Guidance'.

It offers fifteen pointers which, though in themselves are no 'panacea to all ills' do provide a yardstick for investigation. These are as follows:

1. If gifts are used to promote the project be cautious.
2. Watch the vendor's claims for investment.
3. Carefully consider extra costs, sometimes termed closing costs, progress commissions or financing arrangements.
4. Be particularly alert to the fees and arrangements for management and maintenance and how they could increase over the life of the timesharing. In particular, check whether there are funds for major refurbishments and repairs.
5. How frequently will the accommodation be refurbished and how many other weeks will be unlet for annual maintenance?
6. Check that annual maintenance charges include insurance cover for the cost of comparable accommodation if, for whatever reason, the unit is unavailable for your use.
7. Do not surrender to pressure.
8. Remember that the exchange arrangements with other timesharers in other places cannot be guaranteed.
9. Enquire into the track record of the vendor, the developer and the management company.
10. Be particularly careful if building, equipping or furnishing of the timeshare properties and 'promised' ancillary facilities are not complete.
11. Be very careful to find out precisely what your rights are if the builder or the management company has money troubles or in some way defaults.

12. Make sure you have a written contract signed by all parties.
13. Make sure that the vendor is the owner and if the vendor is not the owner be absolutely satisfied as to who is the owner of the freehold. Make absolutely certain that there is not a mortgage on the property.
14. Take special care that you are buying from an existing timeshare owner.
15. Have it spelt out beyond misinterpretation, the actual period during which you, the purchaser, will be entitled to occupy the premises each year.

The leaflet goes on to provide amplification of the points made in some detail and though you will place your individual interpretation on these comments in the light of your contact with the developer/vendor, it should lead you, all else being in order, to a conclusion good or bad.

It is amazing how, with the first burst of sunshine and the glare of dazzling white stucco, even the basic cautions are thrown to the winds. Most timeshares are honestly offered and fairly presented so that if simple basic rules are followed the timesharer will end up entirely happy and bursting with goodwill.

You would never, however, buy a used car without the most stringent examination of the service history, the previous owner, the mechanical condition, bodywork, tyres and general overall condition.

Finally you would test drive it thoroughly and pay particular attention to the after-sales services offered plus whatever guarantees were available.

I have used the car analogy since most timeshare purchases are approximately equal to the value of a used car. Now imagine the purchaser who walks into the showroom, walks around the outside of the vehicle, produces his cheque book, writes a cheque and drives away.

Never, you may cry, but so many timeshares are bought in such a way and naturally a small percentage of these will be unhappy, leaving them to seek redress through the machinery provided by the laws of the country.

These laws will differ greatly and if you want to make a serious study of the subject then you will find James Edmonds' *International Timeshare* (2nd edn) of enormous interest and help.

Mostly however you will find that the onus is on you the buyer and as always it is a question of 'Let the buyer beware.'

Within the UK there are numerous Acts in operation which afford protection for the consumer and in this respect we are better served than most countries.

We have, for example, a Consumer Protection Advisory Committee and provision is made under the Act governing this to refer any infringement to this committee covered by these general provisions.

Consumer trade practice under the Fair Trading Act 1973 means any practice which is for the time being carried on in connection with the supply of goods (whether by way of sale or otherwise) to consumers or in connection with the supply of services and consumers and which relates:

1. to the terms or conditions (whether as to price or otherwise) on or subject to which goods or services are sought to be supplied; or
2. to the manner in which those terms or conditions are communicated to persons to whom goods are or are sought to be supplied;
3. to promotion (by advertising, labelling or making of goods, canvassing or otherwise) of the supply of goods or of the supply of services; or
4. to methods of salesmanship employed in dealing with consumers; or
5. to the way in which goods are packed or otherwise got up for the purpose of being supplied; or
6. to methods of demanding or securing payment for goods or services supplied.

Subject to sections 15 and 16 of this Act the secretary of state or any other minister or the director may refer to the Advisory Committee the question whether a consumer trade practice specified in the reference adversely affects the economic interests of the consumers in the United Kingdom.

Knowing your rights is however only half the battle and you would be most unwise to embark on any legal action without qualified representation. It might though be enough to unnerve any glib salesman and force him (or her) to deal in fact rather than fiction.

Since writing this chapter the Department of Trade and Industry have produced an excellent booklet *Your Place in the Sun – or Is It?* which is more or less repeating the English Tourist Board's advice. Copies are available upon request from the Department of Trade and Industry, Consumer Affairs Division, 10–18 Victoria Street, London, SW1 ONH (Tel. 01–215 3344).

Further updates on the Timeshare Developers Association (see p. 143) are also needed now that it is more firmly established. It is envisaged that the association will eventually represent probably two thirds of the companies selling to the British timeshare market. These will all be bound by a strict code of ethics on every aspect of their operations. Applications for entry will be vetted by a team of lawyers before being put to the Council for approval and both existing and potential timesharers should take heart from this new move which can only benefit the industry as a whole. Their address is on p. 168. Chief Executive of the TDA is Colonel Geoffrey Gilhead.

21 *The Developers' Overview*

For each developer who *has* entered the volatile timeshare market there are probably three times the number who have thought about it long and hard and passed it by. The proposition is after all a pretty daunting one since it involves finding the ideal site, building the apartments, lodges or villas and creating the amenities needed to ensure success.

The market is highly sceptical about artists' impressions so few developers who have yet to establish a track record in this field would be venturesome enough to commence the selling operation until something of a tangible nature is visible. Only then can the developer be sure that the first steps in the credibility stakes have been made.

This assumes of course that the developer is starting from scratch and on a virgin site, but it could be that the developer is adapting an existing structure such as a hotel or old manor house which can either lessen or aggravate his problems according to the age and design of the property.

Hotels have been developed for timeshare because they have problems with occupancy levels during the winter months and look to the timesharer to fill that gap.

After all, if there are sixty or seventy timesharers in residence every week of the year it is a certainty that the hotel's cash flow is going to benefit since, contrary to the popular belief, timesharers as with most of us do not like to cook while on holiday and the luxury kitchens that come with their timeshare apartments or suites are the most under-utilized amenity of the lot.

Instead the timesharers can be found in the bars and

restaurants with the other guests but spending more freely since they at least do not have a hotel bill to pay at the end of their stay for accommodation.

When hotels began to develop timeshare in about 1975 this was an unexpected bonus which the hotel developer had not anticipated. Given the same opportunity today the hotel developer would probably not spend the £7,500 or so on such lavish kitchens but supply instead a more simplified kitchenette facility.

The developer who on the other hand decides to convert a grand old house to timeshare is probably the owner who has embarked on this course because of the crippling overheads which they have to face each year, brought about by a crumbling façade, dry rot, rising damp and the hundred and one problems that make it impossible to fund the cost of upkeep from available family resources.

Timesharing part or all of the property seems both an acceptable and a profitable way of retaining the family interest. It does however call for a massive investment at the outset since it is most unlikely that any baronial hall was designed with timeshare in mind.

Developers have to preserve the character of the place with period decor and furnishing, while providing restaurants, bars, health spas and sporting amenities to attract the timesharer who has come to expect all of these – and more.

Frequently too the number of units that can be created within the property itself is inadequate to sustain the viability of the project and this means chalets or lodges in the grounds but sensibly joined to the main building by covered walkways.

The developer who starts with a virgin site has to face the cost of the land and all building costs so that the initial outlay could (and does) run into several millions before any money is earned.

The time factor is important since the developer is facing heavy finance costs and the sooner the selling process can start the better.

Equally it is a high-risk situation since all it takes is a media campaign to discredit the timeshare 'up the road' and, whatever the rights or wrongs of the situation the developer becomes automatically associated in people's minds with the bad publicity, and nothing dries up the flow of enquiries quicker than 'bad press'.

So what about the returns? No developer enters this market without a prospect of a good financial return. Let us look first at a hotel which has been partly converted to timeshare.

If a hotel has a hundred rooms the decision might have been taken to convert forty to timeshare since this would enable the hotel to retain its identity as a hotel, which is an important feature for the potential timesharer who wants to be able to enjoy all the hotel's existing amenities and yet be able to retreat into the privacy of his or her self-contained luxury suite.

It becomes a 'back-to-back' proposition in that the hotel needs the timesharer to help defray its overheads through better utilization of the amenities while the timesharer needs these same amenities to supplement the facility purchased.

To minimize the disturbance in terms of bricks and mortar the hotelier will have chosen a separate wing or annexe, still an integral part of the superstructure but sufficiently separate to avoid disturbing the comfort of the existing hotel guests while the conversion programme is under way.

There are benefits in costs terms too since minimum building alterations also go hand in glove with minimal building costs.

The time factor is also reduced and within eight weeks the first suite will have been created and a model exists on which future sales can be based.

Since all of the hotel's amenities are already operational it does mean that the selling operation can begin immediately and after six weeks or so the project becomes self-financing.

Generally speaking a property sold on a timeshare basis will produce three times its value and therefore the faster it sells the quicker the return on investment. Once sold there is an immediate profit for the developer and the future costs of maintenance come from out of the management fees.

Seen against normal hotel trading profits of ten per cent

net, a hotelier can, within three years of timeshare selling, achieve the same profit that would otherwise take thirty to forty years.

Of course the hotel is selling off its asset value for a while but this reverts to the hotel after the period of the licence so, although it might be outside the life span of the present owners, the property retains its original asset at an increased value because of the conversion from rooms to suites, which will have been maintained to luxury levels throughout the period of the licence.

Naturally this has not gone unnoticed and we can anticipate the emergence of more hotel-based timeshare in the future.

As we have already seen, the developer wishing to convert all or part of an old country house for timeshare use must be very clear about his or her ultimate objectives.

It has already been demonstrated that apartments within the building itself are infinitely preferable to lodges or chalets or villas in the grounds simply because, like the hotel, the house tends to be the hospitality centre and for those seeking action that's where it all happens.

Of course there can be quite a differential in pricing which would place those apartments within at a premium and as a marketing strategy this could serve to deflect the disappointment of those who were too late to buy in the main building – they can console themselves with 'Well, we didn't have to pay as much.'

In all but the convenience factor of course they are probably better off, since they will be occupying up-to-date accommodation and not suffering the vagaries of Victorian plumbing and all else that goes with older properties.

Mostly these country houses are in remote locations and it follows that to sustain the timesharers' interest the development must be created as a country club with nice restaurants, fully equipped health spas, large recreational areas and adjoining sports facilities.

Because that little extra is called for these developments are more costly to convert and run: after all, staff will have to be brought in daily from neighbouring villages and deliveries of supplies will often entail a premium because of frequency and distance.

The developer also faces constant battles with the local rural district and county councils for suitable planning permissions since they (not having to pay the bills) liked the place very much as it was. When it all comes together however the project usually attracts a great deal of support but the pay-back on investment is a long time in coming.

The virgin site development is probably undertaken by the larger companies who have an established track record and are therefore in the happy position of selling 'off the drawing-board'.

It is perhaps no accident that prominent in this field are such companies as Wimpey and Barratts, the latter now credited with sales of more than £1M per week.

Others with the funds to be able to finance these types of operations are P & O who, having taken over European Ferries, have inherited the La Manga project, where reportedly £16M will be spent over the next few years on the creation of a 5-star hotel, a new third golf course (under the supervision of the Ballesteros brothers – Manuel and Sevriano) and eighty-plus linked villas.

Then there is the McInerney company who are active in the Algarve with the Quinta de Lago project, the R. M. Douglas/Kenning Motor Group who are creating Lakeland Village as a joint venture, and of course the Stakis hotel group.

Many more will emerge as the profits from the industry become too attractive to ignore and to a large extent the industry can draw on this sort of strength for its future credibility.

For the majority however it places the onus of achieving a rapid sell-out on the sales force engaged and often the pressures on the developer are reflected in over-zealous attempts to close the sale. Clearly such recently reported tactics are inexcusable and call for a rethink of policy on the part of some developers, but voluntary restraint will ultimately have to give way to regulation and legislation.

Specialist design skills too are needed and happily there are companies such as Interior Motives International of Southampton who are capable of turning developers' dreams into reality.

22 My Lifestyle – How Will It Be Affected?

Those of us with enough years under our belt will remember that holidaying used to be such a simple affair. You chose the time of the year you wanted to go (or could go), booked your hotel, be it in this country or abroad, made your transportation arrangements and went.

Alternatively, according to your circumstances, you purchased a holiday home, either in the UK or abroad, and went there when you could.

Circumstances have changed all that: the cost of travel has made people look more closely at package tours and the risk of vandalism has made owners fearful of the consequences of leaving property unattended for too long.

In the latter case finding a reliable (and honest) managing agent to let the property has brought the twin problems of accelerated wear and tear on furnishing and fittings plus the lingering doubts about the competence and integrity of the managing agent.

Too many owners have had the experience of telephoning their holiday homes at times when the agent has claimed that he or she has been unable to let, only to have the telephone answered by someone in residence.

When challenged the agent often says that it was only for one night while waiting to move in to another apartment, cottage or villa!

How do you disprove this since you can be sure the occupant has been warned now against answering the telephone and is perhaps being a party to the deception by receiving a reduced rate?

One owner was so incensed that he flew the next day to

Tenerife and confronted the agent after discovering a party of six in occupancy. The occupants had been there two weeks already and had another two weeks to run but the agent said that they had only moved in that day for two weeks.

It is all a question of trust – who can you and who do you in these matters?

The traditional two weeks with the family at an English seaside hotel has given way to more frequent short breaks of three to four days while more and more have seen self-catering apartments as the way to an economical family holiday.

Where holidays abroad are involved this has been, at least until now, the domain of the package-tour operators who have fought vigorously for an ever-increasing share of the market which is now dominated by the larger tour operators – Thomsons, Horizon and Intasun.

This and the self-catering market is now coming under increasing threat from timeshare and, although the numbers are not yet significant to make any appreciable dent in their revenue, it is rapidly growing and cannot be ignored. Predictably then we can expect to see some of the larger tour operators emerging as timeshare developers in due course.

In the main, timeshare offers luxury standards of accommodation – consistently. This, together with a resort offering every amenity such as modern health spas, restaurants, shops, swimming pools, sporting concessions and entertainment for the whole family, gives the holiday maker a chance to enjoy a lifestyle hitherto beyond his or her expectations.

Also if it is an integral part of a luxury hotel then they will enjoy all the services of the hotel at no less favourable terms than normal hotel guests.

This may mean 24-hour room service, porterage on arrival and departure, telex, telephone and secretarial services, dinner parties served by the hotel staff in their suite, laundry and dry cleaning, daily maid service, baby-sitting, access to bars, health spas, games rooms and a host of other services which only come with high-class hotels.

Such standards are not available on package tours or, if they are, then only at costs which few can afford. Timesharers may return to the same place year in year out and if they tire of all this luxury then they can exchange at minimal costs, into a new location offering similar standards in any of 2,000 resorts in over fifty countries.

All this for a 'one-off' payment up front with nothing more to pay except their annual management fees at their own resort and the cost of transportation.

Package tours cannot compete with this while whole ownership of a second holiday home is usually undertaken in the expectation of frequent visits by all the family but quickly becomes a twice-in-the-year visit with no alternative choice. Experience has shown that most people tire of having to visit the same place all the time, which perhaps explains why so many holiday homes are up for sale after 8–10 years.

With timeshare the pattern appears to be that owners visit their 'home' resort in four consecutive years before exchanging and when they exchange they repeat the experience every third and fourth. The attraction however is the flexibility of choice that timesharers have and it is not surprising that many new timesharers are former owners of a second holiday home.

Frequently a developer is asked by a potential timesharer to explain the impact on a timesharer's lifestyle. Many can see the obvious economies involved but fear a catch somewhere.

If a developer is totally honest he will acknowledge the timesharer's worries and say: 'Timeshare calls for a commitment to a period of time at either your resort or in the resort into which you exchange each year, and invariably at the same time.

'It therefore introduces a new discipline in your life and you must be prepared to accept it – the alternative being that you can let it, let friends or family use it, or bank it on the exchange club accumulator for the following year.

'You may need to alter your lifestyle to accept this discipline but it is a small price to pay for all the benefits you will receive.'

Put like this the timesharer is able to grasp the

implications and is then in a position to evaluate. For most an enforced commitment of this nature is a blessing in disguise since it means they must take it up or lose out.

Executives find it particularly welcome since it makes them take a holiday when the likelihood is that without it they would probably work on. Diaries are marked up boldly at the beginning of the year and the period defended determinedly as the year passes.

Many an owner of a small business has been grateful for their timeshare break and undoubtedly their health may have suffered without it.

The club atmosphere that timeshare also creates fosters lifelong relationships with other timesharers occupying the same weeks and social circles grow as a result. So the sharing is not restricted to property but extends into other interests, likes and dislikes, experiences shared and communal moments enjoyed.

True, most timesharers enjoy their privacy and nobody intrudes, but others like to mix and welcome the companionship that this way of life offers.

They say that holiday friendships never last and although that is largely correct a timeshare ownership does throw people into contact more regularly and it is through this that lasting relationships develop.

Some have gone into business together and there are reports of intermarriage between families who met while timesharing so that this integration is all the time contributing to the solid backing for the concept that one meets now at every turn.

Travel broadens the mind but it also brings in its wake a certain status and it would be fair comment to say that many timesharers, whether they have purchased in the UK or abroad, are able through the exchange club facilities, to spend their holidays this year in Hawaii or Fiji or the Bahamas, next year in Acapulco or Rio de Janeiro or Pattaya, and the year after that maybe New Zealand.

Timeshare then can be the key that opens many doors: it offers horizons which normally would be unthinkable for the average person – the world can truly become their oyster.

Nobody can force you to buy and, if you have any

doubts at all, then don't. The better resorts may be judged by their low key (almost 'laid-back') approach and they will see their task as helping you firstly to decide if timeshare is right for you and then, if it is, in making the choice of time, period and size of unit that is most compatible and within your budget.

Do not be surprised if your choice is governed more by availability than anything else. Even so, do your research carefully and do not be rushed: a good prestigious resort will have the patience of Job.

Be suspicious of any discounts offered and do get your solicitor to check any agreements before you sign. If you pay a deposit be sure that this is fully refundable without penalty at any time up to actual completion.

The better resorts will probably state in writing that your deposit will not be banked for ten days and normally they will bank both your deposit and the balance cheque at the same time.

Be sure that your management fees are geared to retail price index RPI throughout the period of the licence and not just for the first 3–5 years.

Finally your instincts will tell you when all is right: be guided by these and do not accept any unduly lavish hospitality during your assessment which might affect your judgement.

Much has already been published on the subject of timeshare and often a great deal is misleading. All too often a features editor of some national newspaper or magazine will decide that it is time they carried an article on the subject, and a freelance writer is engaged to write it.

Deadlines are normally very tight and the time therefore available for proper research is restricted. The end result is that one or two resorts are visited and the article appears based primarily on the writer's impressions and the information picked up from his or her contacts at the resort.

The public at large still tend to believe what they see in print and therefore it is not surprising that they quickly become confused by these conflicting reports. In all probability it is the writer's first contact with the industry and he or she should be the last to claim any expertise.

Unfortunately, they write with an air of authority and

because they are good at their job their articles have impact and influence so that their readers assume, quite wrongly, that they are very knowledgeable and even possibly experts in this field.

Indeed, as I write there is an article in front of me written by a freelance journalist, with presumably no previous experience of the industry, for a widely circulated magazine with a readership of over 100,000 largely professional people. Yet the statistics quoted are clearly plucked out of the air and courses of action are recommended to the potential timesharer without any evidence of deeper involvement to support them.

Naturally no writer of such articles is going to say at the outset, or even later, that they know nothing about this industry and that they are only doing it to earn a crust. They leave it to the reader to presume – and what the reader presumes is entirely up to them.

Timeshare, to conclude, is neither a miracle nor a myth but an excitingly new way of life which is there to be enjoyed by all – assuming basic precautions have been taken and that you are satisfied that it is a way of life for you and your family.

Hopefully this book may have guided your steps. If so it will have proved a worthwhile investment. The market is still young and there will be many exciting developments to come. Timeshare – in whatever ultimate form – is here to stay and you can, if you wish, be part of it.

23 Questions and Answers

Q   We have been considering timeshare for some years but cannot decide between the UK and overseas. What do you advise?

A   If you are going to be holidaying abroad on a regular basis then it makes sense to buy overseas. On the other hand if you intend to holiday only occasionally abroad then buy in the UK and use the exchange club facilities.

Q   We have a daughter of twelve and need to buy during school holidays. Later we may want to change to another period to avoid the crowds. Will it be possible to 'trade in' our week at our own resort?

A   This will depend on the weeks your resort will have left at that time. You may of course find that someone wishes to resell and for a period you may have to purchase to secure this before you have disposed of your own week. Perhaps you should buy two weeks initially and then dispose of one when you no longer need it – the appreciation should yield a profit sufficient to offset the extra cost.

Q   We are confused by the varying periods on offer for timeshare and cannot reconcile these in value terms. Can you help?

A   Your timeshare can be anything from twenty years to perpetuity and usually the number of weeks sold in the project is your best indicator of perceived values. A good tip is: whatever period you opt for, plan the first ten years around your anticipated family situation. Beyond this you have to regard as the unknown and any planning is largely speculative.

Q   Is there a limit on the number of weeks I may buy?

A   This will be limited only by availability and the size of your bank account.

Q   Why is there such a huge differential in the UK between the price of winter and summer weeks when the accommodation and amenities do not vary?

A   The answer is basically that this has been governed by the weather factor but as more and more resorts become all-weather resorts we can expect to see less of a gap in future pricing structures.

Q   Apart from the purchase price what other expenses are there?

A   There is an annual management fee which in most resorts is geared to the cost of living. As a rough guide this is around £100 for each week owned. Beyond this there are travel costs and expenditure on meals and entertainment.

Q   What happens if I cannot take up my week(s) due to illness or changed circumstances?

A   Your resort is geared to let it for you if given enough notice or alternatively you may bank it with RCI (Resort Condominium International) if time allows and take two weeks the following year on an exchange. There are also insurance companies who will insure you against loss of holiday.

Q   Does timeshare purchase represent an investment?

A   In holiday terms, yes, since clearly you will enjoy many years of holidays which will have been secured at today's prices. It is therefore a cushion against inflation.

   In property terms much will depend on what and

where you have bought, but even so your holding is likely to appreciate over the years and this, coupled with the number of free holidays enjoyed after the capital recovery level, will almost certainly show you a profit.

Q   Are there easy payment terms available?

A   Each resort will have its own schemes to offer but there are numerous financial plans to be had, including pay-back schemes geared to whole-life policies which, over a ten-year period, pay back bonuses in excess of the purchase price. APR is currently 13.9 per cent.

Q   What insurance cover do I need in case of damages in my apartment or villa during occupancy?

A   Most resorts cover you fully – not only against accidental breakages but also in respect of third-party liability, plus of course overall coverage on the superstructure itself. Some even cover you against loss of holiday to the extent of the letting value if for any reason your apartment/villa is not available for your use.

Q   How do I know my apartment/villa will be properly looked after when I am not there?

A   Your own assessment of the management you meet will be a fair guide but all resorts exist on the strength of their management team. Next to location, management is everything.

Q   What happens if I want to sell?

A   Your management company can usually arrange to sell your holding (expect a charge of around 10 per cent) or you are free to sell it direct. Generally it is better to let the resort sell it since most keep a register of buyers and they are closer to the market.

Q   Is it automatically inherited by my family if I bequeath it as part of my estate?

A   Perhaps 'automatically' is too sweeping, when one recognizes that certain countries have restraints in this area but if you include it in a will (make sure of this in Spain) there should be no problems.

Q   As a timesharer will I qualify for discounts at the resort or on travel arrangements?

A   Some resorts do offer discounts to their timesharers on drinks and meals while the exchange clubs have affiliation with tour companies who make travel concessions. Hotels however do not normally discount since it only complicates the status of hotel guests who visit more frequently.

Q   How do I know my investment will be secure?

A   You do not, and therefore you should only buy from those companies who have an established reputation and a checkable track record. *Caveat emptor* (Buyer beware) applies as much to timeshare as it does to buying any property – be guided by your instincts by all means but take every reasonable precaution just the same.

Q   What happens in the event of a change of ownership of the development?

A   Much will depend on the wording of your agreement. Most will have a clause which will make it a condition of sale that should the development change hands then the new owner will give an undertaking to honour the covenants entered into by the previous owner with the timesharers throughout the remaining period of the agreement. Effectively this becomes a condition of sale and is enforceable under law.

Q   What happens if the developer goes bust?

A   There is little or no protection against this eventuality

Choosing Your Timeshare

and this is another reason why you should do your homework before you buy. A receiver may be appointed and if so a rescue operation may be mounted.

If the project is nearly sold out then the timesharers may be able to take over the running of the project but there is no hard and fast formula for dealing with this situation.

Q   How do I deal with troublesome neighbours?

A   Your agreement will probably contain a code-of-conduct section and all in residence will be expected to abide by the rules. If a neighbour is being unreasonable then perhaps politely telling them will be enough. If not then you should ask the management to deal with it – they have the right and the authority.

Q   How do I let to friends on a commercial basis?

A   Unfortunately friends and relations tend to take advantage of their privileged status and may expect a 'freebie'. It is better in the interests of harmony not to let to people you know well by making it clear that you bought it as an investment and the revenue you get from letting is part of the realization of that investment.

You are sunk the moment you give in on this as anyone who has ever owned a holiday home can tell you – it is often the reason they sold it.

Q   I understand that I automatically become a member of a local golf club with free golf for up to four persons when I buy timeshare at ——. Is this true?

A   That might well be true but check it out before you buy since the small print sometimes says 'in the first three years' and with golf memberships now costing anything up to £5,000 in the Costa del Sol it would be a shame if you only bought it for the golf facility and could not afford the fees later.

Q Is there in timeshare an association such as the Mediterranean Property Association which will look after the timesharers' interests?

A Not as yet but it is only a question of time before we see the emergence of such a body independent of any of the developers' groupings. Certainly one is badly needed.

Q How can I research the market effectively before I buy?

A You have made a good start in buying this book but may I suggest that you send for brochures from those resorts that have most appeal, then select three that come closest to your requirements. Next visit all three, staying overnight if you are able, leaving the one that attracts you most until last.

Make your choice based on your instincts and from what you have learned from this book.

Appendices

Useful Addresses

Sources of Advice

Tourism Advisory Group Ltd
4/5 Shilling Street
Lavenham, Sudbury
Suffolk CO10 9RH
Tel. 0787 310749 &
    0787 313424

The English Tourist Board
Dept. D
4 Grosvenor Gardens
London SW1W 0DU
Tel. 01-730 3400

Homes Abroad (magazine)
246/248 Great Portland St
London W1N 6DS
Tel. 01-387 7878

Interior Motives International   Interior design specialists
(The Design Business
   Associates)
Shamrock Quay
Southampton
Hants S01 1QL
Tel. 0703 225478

Sources of Advice

The Law Society
(Notaries Organization)
The Law Society's Hall
113 Chancery Lane
London WC2A 1PL
Tel. 01-242 1222

Primeshare International   Specialize in timeshare resales
Hadleigh
Ipswich IP7 5BR
Tel. 0473 824133

The Timeshare Bourse   Timeshare resales and rentals
Tourism Advisory Group
Westminster Bank Chambers
Market Hill
Sudbury,
Suffolk CO10 6EN
Tel. 0787 310755

Timeshare Developers
   Association
4 Old Park Lane
London W1Y 3LJ
Tel. 01-221 9400

Timeshare Developers Group
c/o The Communication
   Group PLC
2 Queen Anne's Gate
   Buildings
Dartmouth Street
London SW1H 9BP
Tel. 01–222 7733

Timeshare Trustees   Timeshare trust company
   (International) Ltd   acting for owners and
PO Box 10   developers
Tower Street Centre
Ramsey
Isle of Man
Tel. 0624 813571

Sources of Advice

Dept. of Trade and Industry
Timesharing Leaflet
Consumer Affairs Division
10–18 Victoria Street
London SW1 0NH
Tel. 01–215 3344

Exchange Clubs

Interval International
Standbrook House
2–5 Old Bond Street
London W1X 3TB
Tel. 01–499 7383

RCI Europe Ltd
Parnell House
19–28 Wilton Road
London SW1V 1LW
Tel. 01–821 6622

Marketing Companies

Carnbrook Timesharing Ltd Marlowes House Tandridge Road Warlingham Surrey CR3 9LS Tel. 01–660 6600	Spain, South of France, UK and French ski resort
Carrick & Co. The Commons Shaftesbury Dorset SP7 8JU Tel. 0747 4001	Yacht timesharing, South of France
Comser International Ltd Fairview Road Timperley Cheshire WA15 7AR Tel. 061–904 9750	Spain and France, and Hapimag

Marketing Companies

International Property Marketing 37 East Street Horsham Sussex RH12 1HE Tel. 0403 56191	Studios and bungalows in Lanzarote and Tenerife
Island Timeshare Ltd 17 Crook Log Bexleyheath Kent DA6 8DZ Tel. 01-301 2838	Almeria and Majorca
Oldway Group Oldway House Castle Street Merthyr Tydfil Wales CF47 8UX Tel. 0685 2386	Hillesdon Court Torquay
Project 81 (Apartments) Ltd Rex Buildings Alderley Road Wilmslow Cheshire SK9 1HY Tel. 0625 530549	Puerto Cabopino Spain
David Scott Int. Services Deerhurst House Epping Road Roydon, Harlow Essex CN19 5RD Tel. 027 979 2162	Apartments, villas and boat timesharing, UK, France, Algarve, Spain, Barbados, Florida, Tenerife
Villa Owners Club Ltd Kentford Lodge Newmarket Suffolk C88 7PT Tel. 0638 660066	Holiday Property Bond

Kenneth Ward & Co.
Exchange House
77 Laleham Road,　　　Apartments, villas and boat
Staines　　　　　　　　　timesharing UK, France,
Middx. TW18 2EA　　　　Holland, Spain, Barbados,
Tel. 0784 64152　　　　　Florida, Seychelles

Developers

Allen House
Allen Street
London W8 6BH
Tel. 01–491 2677

Barnham Broom Golf & Country Club
Barnham Broom
Norwich NR9 4DD
Tel. 0605 45 393

Barratt Multi-Ownership & Hotels Ltd
6 Half Moon Street, Mayfair
London W1Y 7RA
Tel. 01–629 2731

Blakeney Timeshare
Blakeney, Nr. Holt
Norfolk SG4 9BL
Tel. 0462 31771

Brantridge Park
Balcombe, Haywards Heath
West Sussex R17 6JT
Tel. 0444 400235

Broome Park
Barham, Canterbury
Kent CT4 6QX
Tel. 0227 831701

Carvynick Cottages
Summercourt, Newquay
Cornwall TR8 5AF
Tel. 0872 51716

Developers

Carlton Timeshare
Carlton Hotel
East Overcliff
Bournemouth BH1 3DN
Tel. 0202 22011

Cherry Orchard Aparthotel
Station Road
Port Erin
Isle of Man
Tel. 0624 833811

Clowance
Clowance House
Praze-an-Beeble
Camborne
Cornwall RE14 OPT
Tel. 0209 831111

Comben Group Ltd
1 Portland Square
Bristol BS2 8RR
Tel. 0272 425001

Connemara Country Club
Leam, East Recess
County Galway
Eire
Tel. 010 353 572 822790

Coylumbridge Highland Lodges Club
Coylumbridge, Aviemore
Inverness-shire
Scotland PH22 1QN
Tel. 0479 810673

Court Barton
South Huish
Nr. Kingsbridge
South Devon TQ7 3EH
Tel. 0548 561919

Developers

Craigendarroch
Braemar Road
Ballater
Aberdeenshire
Scotland AB3 5XA
Tel. 0338 55558

Dalfaber
Dalfaber Estate
Aviemore
Scotland DA22 1ST
Tel. 0479 810340

De Vere Mews
Canning Place
London W8 5AA
Tel. 01–491 2677

Devoncourt
Douglas Avenue
Exmouth
Devon EX8 2EX
Tel. 0395 272277

Elmers Court Timeshare and Country Club
Lymington
Hants SO4 8ZB
Tel. 0590 76011

Elliott Property & Leisure Group Ltd
31 George Street
London W1R 9FA
Tel. 01–491 2677

Fitzpatrick Castle Holiday Homes
Killiney
County Dublin
Eire
Tel. 0001 851533

Developers

Forest Hills Estate
Kinlochard, Aberfoyle
Stirling
Scotland FK8 3TL
Tel. 08777 278

Heritage Timeshare, Torquay
The Heritage Hotel
Shedden Hill
Torquay
Devon TQ2 5TY
Tel. 0803 24449

Hillesdon Court
Grafton Road
Torbay
Torquay
Devon TQ1 1UR
Tel. 0803 211057

Hunting Gate Group
PO Box 4444
Hitchin
Herts. SG4 OTB
Tel. 0462 34444

Kenmore Club (The)
Kenmore
Loch Tay
Tayside
Scotland W1R 9FA
Tel. 08873 525

Kenning Atlantic Ltd
Vogue House, (Suite 201)
1 Hanover Square
London W1R OEB
Tel. 01–499 8313

Sources of Advice

Keswick Bridge
Lake District Timeshare Lodges
Keswick Bridge Ltd
The Old Station, Station Road
Keswick
Cumbria CA12 4NE
Tel. 076 87 74649

Kilconquhar Castle Estate
Kilconquhar
Elie, Leven
Fife
Scotland KY9 1EZ
Tel. 0333 34501

Kingswear Park
Kingswear
Dartmouth
Devon TQ6 ODA
Tel. 080 425 295

Knocktopher Abbey
Knocktopher
County Kilkenny
Eire
Tel. 010 353 503 57278

La Grande Mare Country Club
Vazon Bay, Castel
Guernsey
Channel Islands
Tel. 0481 56809

Lakelands (The)
Lower Gale, Ambleside
Cumbria LA22 OBD
Tel. 0966 33777

Lakeland Village (The)
Newby Bridge
Ulverston
Cumbria LA12 8PX
Tel. 0448 31144

Developers

Langdale
Great Langdale
Nr. Ambleside
Cumbria LA22 9JD
Tel. 09667 391

Loch Rannoch Highland Lodges
Kinloch Rannoch
Perthshire
Scotland PH16 5PS
Tel. 08822 201

Manor Court
Moretonhampstead
Newton Abbot
Devon TQ13 8RF
Tel. 0647 40859

Marina Village
Nab Wood
Bowness-on-Windermere
Cumbria LA23 3JQ
Tel. 096 62 3233

Marine Quay Club
Cliff Road, Salcombe
South Devon TQ8 8JH
Tel. 054 884 3445

Melfort Club (The)
Melfort House
Kilmelford by Oban
Argyll
Scotland PA34 4XD
Tel. 085 22 257

Moness Country Club (The)
Aberfeldy
Wales
PH15 2DV
Tel. 0887 20446

Developers

Osborne (The)
Meadfoot, Beach
Torquay
Devon TQ1 2LL
Tel. 0803 213311

Quaysiders Club
Borrans Road
Waterhead, Ambleside
Cumbria LA22 OEN
Tel. 0966 33969

Pine Lake Resort
Carnforth
Lancs. LA5 8BR
Tel. 0524 736190

Plas Talgarth
Pennal
Nr. Machynlleth
Powys
Mid Wales SY20 9JY
Tel. 0654 75631

P & O Timeshare Holidays
2–3 Cursitor Street
London EC4A 1LX
Tel. 01–242 5172

Regency Villas at Broome Park
The Broome Park Estate
Barham, Nr. Canterbury
Kent CT4 6QX
Tel. 0227 831771

Rhinefield House
Rhinefield Road
Brockenhurst
Hants SO42 7QB
Tel. 0590 22922

Developers

Scandinavian Village
Aviemore Centre
Inverness-shire
Scotland PH22 1BR
Tel. 0479 810852

Sloane Gardens Club (The)
3 Sloane Gardens
Sloane Square
London W1
Tel. 01–730 0925

Sutton Hall
Sutton-under-Whitestonecliffe
Thirsk
Yorks YO7 2PS
Tel. 0845 579200

St Mellion Golf and Country Club
St Mellion
Nr. Saltash
Cornwall PL12 6RU
Tel. 0579 50849

Stouts Hill
Uley, Nr. Dursley
Gloucestershire
GL11 5BT
Tel. 0453 860321

Swan Timeshare Cruisers
The Swan Hotel
Streatley-on-Thames
Berkshire RG8 9HR
Tel. 0491 873737

Tresco
The Tresco Estate
Isle of Scilly
Cornwall
Tel. 0720 22849

Developers

Walton Hall
Walton
Warwickshire CV35 9HU
Tel. 0789 842424

Wimpey Time Ownership
Springfield Road
Horsham
W. Sussex RH12 2ZA
Tel. 0403 56191

What's on Offer in the UK: Some UK Timeshare Resorts

Resort Location (Developer)	Period of Licence (Years)	Cost Range (High–Low) £	Est'd Since	Management Fee (p.w.) £	No. of Units When Complete
Stouts Hall Gloucestershire Private	80	7,300–1,300	1983	80–87	25
Carvynick Cottages Newquay (Private)	80	6,000–1,000	1978	40–83	28
Marine Quay Club Salcombe (Elliott Property)	80	13,000–3,000	1987	100	N/A
St Mellion, Cornwall (Wimpey PLC)	80	9,200–1,800	1984	125–170	11
Manor Court, South Devon (Manor Court)	40	7,250-1,995 (excl. VAT)	1983	74–87 (excl. VAT)	17
La Grande Mare, Guernsey (Private)	10–33	12,540–1,760 (CI tax free)	1980	50–99	34
Brantridge Park Haywards Heath (Private)	80	10,000–3,500	1982	185	16
Court Barton South Devon (Court Barton PLC)	25	7,000–1,500	1982	166	13
Carlton Timeshare Bournemouth (Carlton Hotels Ltd)	40	12,225–1,650	1982	95–150	14

What's on Offer in the UK: Some UK Timeshare Resorts

Resort Location (Developer)	Period of Licence (Years)	Cost Range (High–Low) £	Est'd Since	Management Fee (p.w.) £	No. of Units When Complete
Elmers Court, Lymington (Barratts)	80	7,900–4,000 (excl. VAT)	1980	75–85 (excl. VAT)	64
Broome Park, Canterbury (Gulf Leisure)	80	5,000–1,000 (excl. VAT)	1981	80–110 (excl. VAT)	40
Coylumbridge Highland Lodges Aviemore (Stakis PLC)	Perpetuity	9,000–2,500	1980	98–113	52
Dalfaber Village Aviemore (Barratts)	Perpetuity	8,000–2,800	1981	95	100
Kingswear Park South Devon (Private)	80	8,150–2,300	1985	85	14
The Lakelands Cumbria (Private)	25	8,100–2,600	1984	105	25
Blakeney, Norfolk (Hunting Gate)	80	5,775–1,250 (excl. VAT)	1982	71–102 (excl. VAT)	5
Lakeland Village Cumbria (R.M. Douglas Kenning Group)	80	10,500–3,800	1984	125	86
Loch Rannoch Scottish Highlands (Barratts)	Perpetuity	7,750–2,600	1976	50–85	85
Plas Talgarth Snowdonia (Barratts)	80	8,950–3,000	1979	85	40
Keswick Bridge, Cumbria (Keswick Bridge Ltd)	80	4,900–1,200	1987	120	N/A
The Osborne, Torquay (Elliott Property)	80	9,800–1,950	1980	99	60
Barnham Broom, Norwich (Private)	77	6,500– 800	1981	84–108	29
Langdale, Lake District (Langdale Partnership)	80	8,750–6,700 (excl. VAT)	1982	114–148 (excl. VAT)	84
Sutton Hall, Thirsk (Private)	80	3,500– 700	1982	100–150	21

What's on Offer in the UK: Some UK Timeshare Resorts

Resort Location (Developer)	Period of Licence (Years)	Cost Range (High–Low) £	Est'd Since	Management Fee (p.w.) £	No. of Units When Complete
Walton Hall Stratford-on-Avon (Private)	25	10,000–4,000 (excl. VAT)	1985	155 (excl. VAT)	81
St Davids Vacation Club Dyfed (Private)	50	4,350–1,150	1983	38–58	17
Craigendarroch Royal Deeside (Private)	Perpetuity	11,000–1,500	1985	42–93	82
Melfort Club, Oban Argyll (Private)	Perpetuity	6,485–2,325 (excl. VAT)	1983	70–100 (excl. VAT)	19
Scandinavian Village Aviemore (Interlude Homes)	93	6,860–2,339 (excl. VAT)	1981	40–54 (excl. VAT)	65
Kilconquhar Castle Fife (Private)	Perpetuity	8,950–3,950	1979	121–152	50
Forest Hills Trossachs (Barratts)	Perpetuity	8,900–3,100 (excl. VAT)	1980	70–90 (excl. VAT)	100
Allen House Club London	30	11,788–9,775	1983	107–145	25

Glossary of Terms and Abbreviations

Accrual Relates to time not used one year which, if deposited with RCI (exchange club) may be used the following year.

Affiliation Refers to association or affiliation with the exchange club (RCI or II).

APR Annual percentage rate.

BPTA British Property Timeshare Association – an alignment of British developers and marketing companies formed to act as the voice of the UK industry.

Club membership A method of selling whereby a club is formed giving members the right to use at specific times. Can also apply to other properties and membership is not specific to any one property.

Colour zones Refers to time divisions used by the exchange clubs.

Co-ownership Usually means that the property is divided into twelfths or less and is a midway point between timeshare and outright purchase (see Multi-ownership).

EHTA European Holiday Timeshare Association. Newly formed to embrace European as well as UK developers.

Exchange club The organization which arranges the exchange. Nearly all major developers are affiliated to either RCI or II – and some to both.

Exchange fee Fees paid by timesharers for administration of exchange by exchange club. Additional to subscription.

Facilities The amenities either on site or near the development such as swimming pools, restaurants, bars, health clubs, shops, cinemas, theatres etc.

Fee simple A US or Canadian term for freehold.

Financing Financial assistance with the timeshare purchase.

Fixed time Time which is purchased for use at the same time each year.

Floating time Usually refers to time purchased in a property which rotates month by month each year but bookings may be made as with a hotel. Many variations of this exist and need to be studied closely.
Freehold Timesharer owns the weeks in perpetuity.
II *See* Interval International.
Inspection visits Viewings arranged by developers usually at subsidized rates.
Interval International The leading rival exchange club to RCI.
Laws governing perpetuity It is forbidden in England and Wales (but not Scotland) for a property to be owned by more than four people for a period exceeding eighty years. Most timeshare in England and Wales is sold on a right-to-use agreement.
Licence agreement The agreement signed between the timesharer and the developer setting out in detail the terms under which the purchase is made and the covenants entered into by both parties.
Limited availability Usually appears in exchange club directories to indicate a resort that is difficult to get into.
Management company Refers to the company which runs the timeshare development post sales. Sometimes a wholly owned subsidiary (preferred) or a separate company given this responsibility.
Management fee Annual fee paid by timesharer to the management company. It should cover everything from cleaning to insurance, taxes and major repairs or replacements.
Membership fee Paid annually as a subscription and sometimes paid by developer for first year. If allowed to lapse then membership ceases. Rejoining may entail subsequent enrolment fee.
Outright sale Means a purchase not of timeshare but of the whole property outright.
Owners committee Formed by the timeshare owners once all timeshare is sold to protect their overall interests.
RCI Resort Condominiums International – the leading exchange club with head office in Indianapolis, USA and branches in Europe.
Resort Refers to the timeshare development.
Right to use by club membership See Club membership.
Right to use by lease Similar to Right to use by licence, but does

Appendices

not usually have the same restrictions on renting. More common in the USA.

Right to use by licence The term usually used to describe time not sold on a freehold basis.

Right to use by stock purchase A method of selling time whereby a limited company owns the property. The timesharer buys stock in relation to the number of weeks owned. Rarely used because of regulations governing limited companies and stock transfers.

RPI Retail price index.

Seasons Time is sold according to high, shoulder, or low season, which in turn are geared to the exchange clubs colour zones. If exchange is the motivation for buying timeshare then particular attention must be given to this aspect. It is not possible to exchange from low or shoulder season into high season even with cash adjustment but high-season owners can opt to exchange into any zone.

Shoulder season Season between high and low season. See also Time divisions.

Spacebank The RCI computer into which your time must be deposited before you can make an exchange. The exchange club will check many things but foremost will be that the resort to which you wish to go has time available and that there are people waiting to come into your resort.

Time divisions These are colour zoned by the exchange club and usually in Europe low season will be November, December (excluding weeks 51–52–1) and January plus part February (coded blue). Shoulder season will be part February, March and April (coded white) while high season will be May–June–July–August–September and most of October plus weeks 51–52–1.

Time period The week(s) an owner has bought in a timeshare development.

Timeshare agent Someone authorized to sell on behalf of the developer.

Timeshare Developers Association The amalgamation of three timeshare groups, The British Property Timeshare Association, The European Holiday Timeshare Association and The Timeshare Developers Group, to form one trade association to serve the interests of both developer and timesharer and to monitor the industry.

Timesharing The purchase of a property only for the weeks you intend to use, the other weeks being bought by other parties. Although you share the property, the weeks you own will be used exclusively by you, your friends, relatives or by those you may authorize from time to time.

Unit The actual property, be it apartment, villa, hotel suite or yacht or anything else that may be bought/sold as timeshare.

Note This Glossary has been compiled with the assistance of *Holiday Timesharing and Travel* now incorporated into *Homes Abroad*.

Typical Timeshare Weekly Rental Rates in a High-class Hotel

Winter Rates (1 Oct.–31 Mar. excluding Christmas and New Year)

Weekly	*Daily*	*(minimum 3 nights)*
£650	£145	1 bedroom sleeping 4
£850	£165	2 bedroom sleeping 6
£1,250	£200	2 bedroom penthouse sleeping 6

Summer Rates (1 Apr.–30 Sep.)

Weekly	*Daily*	*(minimum 3 nights)*
£850	£165	1 bedroom sleeping 4
£1,150	£200	2 bedroom sleeping 6
£1,500	£250	2 bedroom penthouse sleeping 6

Christmas Week (Week 52)

New Year's Week (Week 1)

As per Summer rates.

Since all apartments are fully self-catering if desired, rates are accommodation only.
    Rates are inclusive of management fee and VAT.

Index

Animals, restrictions on, 20, 106
Anti-perpetuity laws, 47-9, 78
Arbitration, 57

Banks, 89-90
Behavioural obligations, 50, 53
Bourse, Timeshare Ltd, 86, 168
British Property Timeshare Association, 143

Calendar, timeshare, 81-4
Changing lifestyle, 153, 154
Charges
   management, 104, 106, 116, 160, 180-2, 184
Club Plan, 48
   committee, casting votes, 65
   committee, election of, 64
   constitution, 60
   holiday certificates, 61
   Meetings, Annual General, 73
   methods of purchase, 48
   obligations
      committee, 66
      holiday certificate holders, 70
      members, 68
Club-style timeshare, 25, 26
Code of Caution and Guidance (leaflet), 144
Code of conduct, 57, 163
Commission
   rentals, 86
   resales, 85-8
Committee
   casting votes, 64

   Club Plan obligations, 66
   election, 64
   owners', 184
Community timeshare, 24
Company purchase, 48
Consumer protection
   Advisory Committee, 146-7
   associations, 142-3
   Fair Trading Act, 146-7
Cooling-off period, 48, 77-9
Co-ownership, 26, 27, 141

Deposits, 76-7, 79
Developers, 148-52, 171-9
   bankruptcy, 162-3
Discounts, 162
Disposal of timeshare, 85-8

English Tourist Board guidelines, 144-5
European Holiday Timeshare Association (EHTA), 143
Exchange
   clubs, 44, 51, 117-23
   summary, 122
   systems, 117-23

Fair Trading Act, 1973, 146
Family considerations, 159
Financial obligations, 52
Financing
   banking facilities, 89
   finance house, 90-1
   in-house, 90
Floating time, 184

Hapimag, 31-2
Holiday
  certificates, 61-3, 67-72, 74
  clubs, 31-2
  comparisons
    hotel, 97-9
    independent travel, 101-3
    package tour, 100, 101
  Property Bond (HPB), 28-30
Homes Abroad (magazine), 86, 167
Hotel based timeshare, 25

Inheritance tax, 94-5, 162
Inspection visits, 91, 127, 130, 137-9
Insurance cover, 105, 161
International Timesharing, 47, 146
Interval International (II), 118, 120, 121
Investment, 21, 160, 162

Land ownership, 49
Law and Property Act, 1925, 49
Law Society, The, 168
Leased timeshare, 47
Legal procedures
  administration, 78
  deposits, 76-7, 79
  documentation, 77, 81
  solicitors, 77-81
Letting, 86, 163
Licence, 51-7
  freely assignable, 19
  right to use, 47, 50
Location, 127-30

Management, 107
  agents and companies, 134-7, 139-41, 184
  agreement, 108-10
  charges, 104, 106, 116, 160, 180-2, 184
Market
  growth, 18
  research, 164, 180-3
  size, 17

Membership fees, 184
  RCI and II, 117-23

Neighbours, 156, 163

Ownership
  change of, 162
  comparisons of benefits, 41
  outright, 21, 22

Packaged holidays
  comparisons, 23
Pets, 20, 58, 106
Purchase, methods of
  club plan, 48
  company, 48
  lease, 47
  licence, 47

Rentals, 86, 187
Resales, 85-8
  summary, 88
Resorts Condominiums International (RCI), 44, 117-23
Right to Use licence
  arbitration, 57
  owner's obligations, 55
  rights assured, 50
  the grant, 51
  timesharers' obligations, 52, 55
Rights, 140-1, 147, 163

Seasons, 185
Self-catering, 43
Selling up, 85-8
Solicitors, 77-81
Spacebank, RCI, 117-23

Tax, 93-6
  capital gains, 95
  inheritance, 94-6
Timeshare
  availability, 169-79, 180-2
  Bourse Ltd, 86, 168
  concept, 43
  customer profiles, 33-5
  definition, 13

Developers Association (TDA), 143, 147, 168, 185
future, 43-4
history, 14-16
image, 36-7
length of term, 159

management, 104-6, 107, 108-15, 134, 137
Time zones, 118, 185

Your Place in the Sun – or is it? (booklet), 147

*Press acclaim for the Robert Hale **Living in** ... series*

LIVING IN FRANCE
'If this book is not on the shelves of every UK national either living, or with a holiday home, in France, then it should be.'
The Law Society's Gazette
'Anyone who is considering buying property, whether on the Riviera or back from the coast, should read *Living in France*.'
Financial Times

LIVING IN ITALY
'Covers everything from law and order to gardening and places of worship.'
Sunday Times
'This book is one of a series from Hale which could be the best investment you could make when leaving these shores.'
Dorset Echo

LIVING IN SPAIN
'Anyone thinking of living in Spain or of buying a holiday home there ought to read this book carefully. The practical help offered cannot be over-emphasized. Mr Reay-Smith seems to have thought of everything.'
The Law Society's Gazette
'Should be the first buy for anyone thinking of buying a property in Spain. It is crammed full of useful facts.'
Homes and Travel Abroad

LIVING IN PORTUGAL
'A well-written, informative book crammed full of fascinating facts and sound advice with a delightful overlay of humour.'
Anglo-Portuguese News